PRAISE FOR
NOTHING LEFT UNDONE

In Nothing Left Undone, author Perpetua Anaele presents a riveting and spell-bounding account of her father's legacy; a full body of virtues and life lessons of hard-work, endurance, perseverance, forgiveness, peace, kindness, and love. Most of all, his legacy of love is re-enforced by references from the Word of God.

The story is riveting, as it begins with lessons from a purposeful and visionary young man, her father; against all odds and draw-backs he had the foresight and wisdom regarding the transformative power of education. His high work ethic and tenacity are displayed in the tremendous number of gruesome tasks that he had to accomplish daily prior to attending school. He accomplished all that he sought and worked for, becoming a teacher, a community leader, and a liaison between missionaries and his community. His journey as a caring husband and nurturing father further leads the reader into the home of this great man. He educated his family with meager resources and did it with dignity. His discipline and life lessons are far-reaching, as I have had the privilege of contact with the author and have seen the depth of her character and integrity.

This book is a legacy of love to an awesome father. It is also an inspirational account of life lessons and an assisting guide for daily living. Mr. Lawrence Nwalozie Nwosu's insights on living a life of peace, love, loyalty to family, virtues of hard-work, discipline, integrity and most of all, an unwavering commitment to God, comes at a time when humanity is in dire need of this wealth of wisdom. I recommend this book as a wonderful inspiration to all.

— **Marilyn Anderson-Boayue**

Nothing Left Undone is an inspiring, powerful, and easy to read memoir. The Author uses stories and experiences with her beloved father in a village in Rivers State, Nigeria, to effectively communicate how to live a simple, fulfilling, honorable, and influential life in a challenging society. The stories and experiences were thrilling and instructive. I enjoyed reading the book, and I hope you do too.

— **Martin Onwu, JD, Ph.D**

Nothing Left UNDONE

A Memoir

PERPETUA ANAELE

authorHOUSE

AuthorHouse™
1663 Liberty Drive
Bloomington, IN 47403
www.authorhouse.com
Phone: 833-262-8899

© 2021 Perpetua Anaele.
All rights reserved.

No part of this book may be reproduced, stored in a retrieval system, or transmitted by any means without the written permission of the author.

Published in the United States by Authorhouse 03/16/2021

ISBN: 978-1-6655-0081-4 (sc)
ISBN: 978-1-6655-0080-7 (e)

Library of Congress Control Number: 2020918313

Print information available on the last page.

This book is printed on acid-free paper.

Because of the dynamic nature of the Internet, any web addresses or links contained in this book may have changed since publication and may no longer be valid. The views expressed in this work are solely those of the author and do not necessarily reflect the views of the publisher, and the publisher hereby disclaims any responsibility for them.

Scripture quotations marked NIV are taken from the Holy Bible, New International Version®. NIV®. Copyright © 1973, 1978, 1984 by International Bible Society. Used by permission of Zondervan. All rights reserved. [Biblica]

Scripture quotations marked KJV are from the Holy Bible, King James Version (Authorized Version). First published in 1611. Quoted from the KJV Classic Reference Bible, Copyright © 1983 by The Zondervan Corporation.

Book design by Hollys and Rejoice Anaele.

To my sweetheart, Dr. Sabinus Fyne Anaele—who believed in and supported me in this endeavor.

&

To my children, Rejoice, Hollys, Beverly, and Jamal Fyne —may you always rise and shine, finding your purpose in life.

Lawrence Nwalozie Nwosu

CONTENTS

Author's Letter to her Late Father................................. xiii
Preface xvii

Chapter 1   An Unforgettable Day................................ 1
Chapter 2   My Worst Nightmare................................. 7
Chapter 3   Hard Work Determines Success................ 20
Chapter 4   Education Is Priceless...............................35
Chapter 5   Dare to Lead.. 52
Chapter 6   Character Matters..................................... 67
Chapter 7   Forgiveness Is Freedom 89
Chapter 8   Cherish Your Family................................109
Chapter 9   Love Is the Greatest of All Gifts...............131
Chapter 10 A Peaceful Heart Is a Healthy Heart........154
Chapter 11 Contentment Is Key to Harmony 167
Chapter 12 Build a Solid Foundation 181

About Nothing Left Undone.......................................191
About the Author...193

ACKNOWLEDGEMENT

I greatly thank God, the Creator of heaven and earth, for giving me life, selecting me, bringing me this far, and enabling me to complete this part of my life journey.

To my mother, Theresa Nwosu—thank you for contributing significantly toward the drafting of this memoir and for giving my siblings and me the gift of life. Like a fruitful vine, you filled our father's table with ten wonderful children and stood by our father to raise nine of us. You are truly a virtuous woman, our father's anchor, and the pillar of our family.

To my brothers, sisters, and other family members —thank you for encouraging me and for praying for me throughout this important journey of my life. May the bond we share remain forever unbroken.

To other remarkable people who supported me throughout this amazing journey- I am profoundly grateful for your friendship and support.

AUTHOR'S LETTER TO HER LATE FATHER

Dear Papa,

Thank you for your tireless efforts in raising my siblings and me. We are who we are today because of your extraordinary dedication to our upbringing. You were the best father anyone could ask for, and I am lucky to be your daughter.

No day goes by since your passing that I don't think about you. I miss you so much and want you to know that you are always in my heart. As I told you repeatedly before you passed, I remain grateful for the sacrifices you made to give me the best things of life. Although you were ninety-eight years old when you passed, your exit on June 1, 2017 was painful and shocking to me. Today, however, I am consoled by constantly telling myself that you are happy and at the right place.

On December 26, 2016 when we last met, you asked that I remember you, and I promised I would. This book is just one of the ways I have chosen to showcase my forever love for you. Through this book, I hope to capture wonderful memories we shared together and wish that whoever reads it can benefit from your life lessons as I have.

My irreplaceable father, I will always love and cherish you. You have left behind positive footprints in the sand of time. Sleep well until we meet again to part no more.

Your lovely daughter,

Perpetua Anaele

DISCLAIMER

The stories in this book reflect the author's personal recollection of events. Dialogue has been re-created from memory, and some names, locations, and identifying characteristics have been changed to protect the privacy of those depicted.

PREFACE

A few years ago, a friend invited me to her church in Mozambique, southern Africa. At the service, a pastor was preaching about our purpose in life. He described a funeral event he had attended, where some dignitaries had lined up to pay their last respects to their deceased colleague. He explained that as he sat and watched, they lauded the achievements of their late colleague, lamenting on how sad it was that they had lost him so soon.

After describing this event, the preacher asked each member of the congregation to picture him or herself being dead and laid in a beautiful casket in front of the pulpit. "While there," he continued, "friends and family members gather to pay you their last respects. What will they say about you? What type of life did you live while you were alive? Will you be remembered as a notorious individual who never got along with people? Will people miss you for the outstanding life you lived on earth? Will some be happy that you are no more? How will you be remembered after your death?"

After the sermon that day, the congregation was silent and emotionally touched. I went home, telling myself that I must live a life full of purpose. I later outlined how to achieve this purposeful life and for months, I did stick to my rules.

A few years later, however, I forgot all about the sermon and became occupied with life's challenges. Then, in 2017, I lost my dear father—a man who worked tirelessly to make me who I am today. During his funeral service, thousands of people gathered at the church to pay him their last respects. Four priests conducted the service that day. As my father's lifeless body lay in a beautiful casket before the pulpit, the priests began praising him for his achievements in life. My oldest brother, Pollycap, also read an outstanding eulogy of him. I sat quietly with my siblings in the front spot at the pew of the church, listening to the great speeches and shedding tears.

Later, I flipped through the pages of my father's funeral event booklet and silently read wonderful eulogies from people whose lives he had positively touched. Immediately, I remembered the preacher's sermon from years ago and began to reflect on the important legacies my father had left. I also came to the realization that nothing my father had envisioned in this world was left undone. He finished his race on earth in a positive way, and it is up to me to do the same.

This book is an attempt to capture some great memories I shared with my father. As you read this book, it is my hope that you ask yourself two simple questions: what is your purpose in this world, and how would you like to be remembered when you are no more? It is my intention that with this book, you can emulate my father through his various life lessons, accomplishing your goals and making positive decisions that can endure the test of time. I wish you all the best as you read this book and pursue a life full of purpose.

CHAPTER 1

AN UNFORGETTABLE DAY

It was a day like any other. I had woken up at 6:30 a.m., gotten the kids ready for school, and departed by train to my job in Washington, D.C. On arriving at work that day, I began my daily activities—turning off my cell phone, getting a cup of coffee, reviewing my packed schedule, and tackling each item of the day. After attending three meetings that morning, I was exhausted and ready for lunch. I took my cell phone from my bag, went to the cafeteria, got my lunch, and stepped outside of the building.

On that beautiful Tuesday afternoon, the sun was out. The sky was clear, and the weather breezy and splendid. "A lovely day," I said to myself.

Sitting under a tree to have my lunch, I turned on my phone to check my email. I was surprised to receive an unusual text message from my sister, Juliet, who lives in nearby Maryland. She had forwarded me a picture from our sister-in-law, Nneka, who was taking care of our father in the village in Nigeria. The picture was of our father, who appeared very sick.

Anxious, I perused the text. Juliet informed me that our father, Mr. Lawrence Nwalozie Nwosu, was very sick but had refused to seek medical attention. "Perpetua," she wrote, "call me as soon as you receive this message."

I could not believe what I was reading. I hurriedly dialed Juliet's phone number, but she did not pick up. I then dialed my father's Nigerian number, hoping and praying that he would pick up the phone.

Suddenly, I heard a voice that sounded like his. "Hello, who's calling?" he asked.

"Papa, is that you? It's me."

"Perpetua, how are you? How are the children doing? And your husband? Have you heard from your siblings? Are you all in peace?"

My father continued his endless questions, as if nothing was wrong. It was typical of him each time I called to first call me by my name and then begin asking me many questions all at once. He would never end without asking whether my siblings and I in the United States were living in peace.

When it became obvious, however, that my father was too excited about my call to stop asking me questions, I gently interrupted. "Papa, we are all doing well. How are you?"

Nothing Left Undone

"Everything is all right, my daughter; we thank God."

"Papa, I don't think all is well with you."

"I am fine. Nothing is wrong."

"I don't think so, Papa. You need to go to the hospital immediately to have the doctors take care of you. From your picture, which Nneka sent today, you have lost some weight," I added.

"Which picture? What are you talking about? I'm fine," he insisted.

I maintained my stance. "No, you are not. Please go to the hospital, so doctors can take care of you."

"Perpetua, you worry for nothing. I'm fine. Don't bother yourself. I am not going anywhere."

After five minutes of unsuccessful efforts to convince my father to go to the hospital, I began to cry. "If you love me as much as you always say you do, Papa, please go to the hospital, so you can be alive for me."

"My daughter, you know I love you. Please don't cry. I'm fine. Please stop crying. You have nothing to worry about. I don't want to go to the hospital." He was adamant.

"Why, Papa? Don't you care about your health? I'm your daughter, and I cannot deceive you. Please go to the hospital.

If you are worried about the expenses, I will send you some money right away. Please go."

There was silence, as if he had hung up the phone.

"Hello, Papa, are you still there?"

"Yes, I'm here," he replied, but he did not say another word.

Having lived with my father for over twenty years before immigrating to the United States, I clearly understood what his silence meant: he did not want to discuss the issue any further. Since we were not getting anywhere on the issue, I began to intensify my weeping, hoping that it would compel him to change his mind.

At that moment, some colleagues, who were having lunch outside, noticed that I was crying. They began to surround me and ask what was wrong. I never responded; instead, I turned off my cell phone and continued to sob. One of them took my hands and said, "Perpetua, take it easy; stop crying. I have never seen you this emotional before. It's well."

But I kept on sobbing without saying a word. Turning to her colleagues, she said, "Let's go back to the office. She needs the moment alone to deal with whatever issue she has. We are obviously making it worse for her. She will be all right."

They left, and I was still crying. After a few minutes, I phoned Juliet again, and this time, she picked up. She was obviously upset that our father had refused to seek medical attention but promised to call him to persuade him to seek help.

Nothing Left Undone

I then hung up and called my mother in Nigeria. When my mother—Theresa Nwosu—picked up, I said, "Nma, how are you? It's me, Perpetua."

"Pepe, my daughter, is everything okay? You sound rather distraught. Are you all right?"

Blowing my nose, I said, "I'll be fine, Nma. Are you aware that Papam is not feeling well but has refused to seek medical care?"

"My daughter, I have tried to persuade him to go to the hospital, but he has remained stubborn. This is uncharacteristic of your father. I will keep talking to him. Maybe with your call, he might change his mind and go to the hospital."

"Please, Nma, do whatever you can to persuade him to go to the hospital. I will be very grateful if you can convince him to go. I have not known Papam to be afraid of seeking care at the hospital. Please keep talking to him. I will call back later to see how he's doing. Have a nice day."

I hung up and began contemplating to travel to Nigeria that weekend to handle the issue myself. Then, I remembered I had already gone on vacation for the year and had used up all my earned leave.

Taking a quick look at my watch, I realized forty-five minutes had passed, and my lunch was over. Without eating a thing, I grabbed my lunch and ran to the office for my one o'clock meeting. Throughout that afternoon, I could

Perpetua Anaele

not function well. I kept remembering my father's situation and my unsuccessful conversation with him about seeking medical care. I kept praying and asking God to change his mind.

As soon as my workday was over, I hurriedly turned off my computer, took my handbag, and rushed out of the building. Outside, I turned on my cell phone, anxious to find out the latest development in persuading my father to seek care. Sure enough, Juliet had texted, informing me that our father had finally decided to go to the city of Port-Harcourt in Rivers State, Nigeria, to seek care.

"Praise God," I shouted, loud enough to cause a pedestrian to stop.

"Ma'am, are you all right?"

"Yes, I'm perfect, thanks for asking."

I kept walking and at times running until I entered the Foggy Bottom Metro Station in Washington, D.C. When I took a seat on the train, I closed my eyes and thanked God for answering my prayers.

At home that evening, I phoned Juliet. She informed me that our father had been admitted into one of the best hospitals in Port-Harcourt and was under the doctors' care. Oh, how relieved I was to hear that good news!

CHAPTER 2

MY WORST NIGHTMARE

The next day, my worst nightmare began. When I called to check on my father, he was in pain. Sister Angela—Sister Ange—one of my sisters, who was taking care of our father in the hospital, took the phone from him and told me that the doctors were running all kinds of tests on him. They could only commence their treatment after the results were out.

"Granted, but what in the world did they do to make Papam's situation worse than it was?" I asked. "When he was in the village, he was eating, talking, and walking. Why is he constantly in pain? Can't they give him some painkillers? What kind of tests are they running that are making his situation worse?"

"Papam will be all right," Sister Ange responded. "You need to be patient for the doctors to complete their testing and diagnose the illness before commencing any treatment. I know you are concerned. We all are as well, but Papam will be all right. Go to work and remember to leave your cell phone on. I will call later to update you on his situation. It's well, Perpetua."

"Sister Ange, please don't forget to call me. I will be checking my phone from time to time. Bye."

I slowly turned off the phone. At work that day, I again could not focus. I kept checking my phone, anxiously expecting some messages.

When my phone rang, it was Sister Ange calling from Nigeria. After we exchanged greetings, I thanked her for calling and asked what was going on.

With a low voice, as if she had been crying, she replied, "Well, Papam is still not feeling well."

I was dumbfounded.

"Hello, Perpetua. Are you still there?"

Clearing my throat to answer, I slowly said, "Yes, I'm here. How bad is his condition?"

"Unfortunately, it's serious. He is still in excruciating pain."

After a moment of silence, I asked, "What do we do now?"

"The doctors have placed him on medication, and he is sound asleep. We will be monitoring his condition carefully. Just pray for him. I will keep updating you from time to time."

Nothing Left Undone

Turning off the phone, I slowly sat on my office chair, not saying a word for about five minutes. Later, I began to shed tears, hoping and praying that my father would recover soon.

Regrettably, a week later, my father's health drastically deteriorated. My siblings who surrounded his hospital bed were praying and hoping that he would get better. I could not understand what was going on. I asked if I could speak to the doctors, but my siblings informed me that the doctors were attending to other patients and could not speak with me at the moment. They assured me, however, that our father would be all right. Sadly, two weeks later, my father's condition was critical.

"If he is not responding to treatment at this hospital, please take him to another hospital," I suggested to my siblings, but they said the doctors were trying their best. I kept wondering why my father would be so sick at a place where he was supposed to heal.

It's clearly ironic, I said to myself. *Don't people get better at the hospital? Why is he getting worse?*

Three weeks later, my father was on oxygen support. "How in the world did this happen? How could this be?" I asked.

At the beginning of the fourth week, when I called to check on my father, he was terribly sick. He could neither recognize my voice on the phone nor speak clearly. "What the heck is going on?" I lamented.

Perpetua Anaele

I hung up the phone and began blaming myself for encouraging my father in the first place to seek care. Perhaps, I reasoned, if he had continued to stay in the village without seeking care at the hospital, his health would not have deteriorated.

My mind began to race with unanswered questions. *What if something bad happens to him now? What will I do?*

Three days later, my phone rang. It was Sister Ange. "Perpetua, Papam has asked to speak with you. In fact, he has spoken to all of our siblings in the United States, and you are the only one he has yet to speak to. I tried calling you several times yesterday but could not reach you. I believe he has an important message for you."

"This is concerning, Sister Ange; this is definitely not good." Gently setting down the dishes I was washing, I added, "Please put him on the line."

While on the phone with my father, there was silence. "Papa, Papa, hello, are you there?" I asked, but he could not say a word. "How are you doing today? Have you eaten? Has the pain gone down a little? Please talk to me, Papa. I heard you have an important message for me. I am here now; please go ahead and talk to me."

There was still silence. I began to wonder if he could not recognize my voice, or if he was upset with me. Perhaps he was calling to remind me why he was initially hesitant about seeking care.

Nothing Left Undone

I continued to speak, calling him the most wonderful father on earth and reminding him of his achievements, especially of his great love for his family. I was probably on the phone with him for ten minutes, but he never said a word. From time to time, I would ask if he could hear me, but he would not respond. Sister Ange in the background, however, would say, "Yes, he hears you. He keeps nodding his head when you ask him a question. Continue, he's listening to you."

Consequently, I continued to speak, letting him know how great of a father he had been, and how much I loved him. After about five more minutes on the phone with him, I began to cry, because I knew from his silence that he had deteriorated terribly. I then started praying for him, asking God to make him feel better.

Later, Sister Ange took the phone from him and told me that he would be all right. She emphasized that he was listening and nodding as I spoke. That was reassuring.

Sister Angela also recommended that I stop bothering myself and pray for him instead. I later asked her what message my father had passed to the rest of my siblings, but she said nothing in particular, adding that he was probably trying to hear our voices.

Turning off the phone, I began to feel guilty for not being at my father's bedside. It pained me so much that he could not recognize my voice or say a word to me. It hurt even more that I could not be with him to remind him in person how much I loved him. That night, uncharacteristic of me, I left my chores undone and went straight to my bedroom to pray to God to heal my father.

The next morning, June 1, 2017, my alarm, which I set at 6:30 a.m., went off, but I was too sleepy to wake up. As the alarm continued, I slowly took a look at the window in my bedroom, and everywhere was unusually dark. Reluctantly, I turned off the alarm and slumped back to my bed, trying to sleep again.

After a few minutes of unsuccessfully trying to sleep, I heard loud thunder from outside, as if my father was rebuking me to wake up and get ready for the day. I jumped out of bed and began to get ready for work. After preparing my favorite breakfast of scrambled eggs, pancakes, coffee, orange juice, and strawberry yogurt, I immediately lost my appetite. I took a sip of my coffee and started heading to work.

The outdoors were cloudy and rainy. Heavy raindrops made huge noises, startling me. I stood in front of my house, speechless. Suddenly, a flash of lightning burst near me and flashed to the opposite side of the building. I rushed back to the house, where I changed my shoes for rain boots and got my umbrella. Then, I began walking down to the Largo Metro Station in Maryland to catch the train to work.

As I walked carefully to avoid falling down, I eyed the sky, hoping it would stop raining. On a normal day, I enjoy the sound of raindrops, but on that day, having seen the sky covered with various shades of gray, I wondered if the heavy and uncontrollable downpour would ever stop. The air was as humid as ever, and there were no birds outside. With the

Nothing Left Undone

sky being strangely dark, all cars had their headlights on. As I waited for cars to pass before crossing the road to the train station, then came crashes of thunder, roaring like a wounded lion. The gloomy nature of the day also reflected in my mood as I began to think about my father's tragic situation. Attributing my sadness to the phone call I had with him the day before, I wondered if he was feeling better.

Is he responding to the treatment now? What about his pain? Should I take off from work today and call home to check on him? These questions and more lingered in my mind as I waited to cross the road. On realizing that I had an important meeting in the office, however, I decided to quicken my pace and enter the train. I arrived at work about fifteen minutes late, and all day I was miserable.

I returned home from work around 7:30 p.m. After taking my shower and getting ready to prepare dinner, I received a call from my husband, who was working at the U.S. Embassy in Dhaka, Bangladesh. Due to the time difference between Dhaka and Maryland, I was not expecting him to call me at that time; he was supposed to be getting ready to go at work. He asked where I was.

"I have just returned home from work, honey, and I'm trying to prepare dinner. How are you, and is everything okay?"

During this phone call, something unusual also happened. The kids were all surrounding me in the kitchen, as if they were expecting me to fall down, or as if something bad had happened.

"The man is gone," my husband said.

A look of confusion played across my face. "Excuse me, which man, and what do you mean, 'gone'?"

"Pet, God has taken your father. He's gone to heaven."

On hearing this, I was speechless.

"Hello, are you there? Pet, speak to me. Are you all right? Hello?"

I gently dropped the phone, slumped on the floor, and began to cry out loud. As I screamed, the kids held me, pleading with me to take it easy.

"How could he be gone? I just spoke with him yesterday. Is this some kind of joke?" I asked.

Still in denial, I ran to my bedroom and called Juliet on the phone. She picked up the phone and was crying. I immediately hung up the phone and called another sister, Ebere, who lives in the United States. She picked up and was crying. Without saying a word, I hung up again and called my brother, Emeka, who is also in the United States. Without any greetings, he said, "Perpetua, Papam is gone. Can you believe it?" I refused to hear that sort of news, so I hung up and called my sister, Beth, who lives in Chicago.

When Beth did not pick up, I finally stopped and came to terms with what I had been dreading.

Nothing Left Undone

I remember saying to myself, "So, this is real. My father is gone, but where did he go to? Does it mean I will not ever get the chance to speak with him? Does it mean I will have to delete his contact information from my phone? Does it mean there will be no one asking me millions of questions at the same time when next I call? Does it mean I will never see him when I visit Nigeria again? Who did he leave with the huge responsibility of taking care of the family? What about my mother? Oh, no, he can't be gone."

I locked the bedroom door and continued crying, asking God why, why, and why until I was too tired to cry.

Then, I began to reflect on the memories I had shared with my father. All I could remember was my last encounter with him on December 26, 2016. The day before, my entire family—my kids, my husband, and I—had flown in to Nigeria to spend Christmas with our loved ones there.

Before this trip, for years, my husband had been visiting my father in Nigeria and reporting back to me on his situation. We had agreed that since I was with the kids in America, and he was alone in Bangladesh, it was better for him to visit my father frequently in Nigeria and report back to me.

For some reason, however, before this December trip, my husband had repeatedly reminded the family to travel to Nigeria to see our families. It had been about fourteen years since the kids last saw their grandparents. In fact, my last daughter, Rejoice, who was twelve at the time, had never seen her grandparents, so the trip was rightly due. Initially, I was hesitant about the idea of six family members making transatlantic trips to Nigeria. My reason was that it was not cost effective for six people to travel there for only four days. Given the constant reminder from my husband of the need for the kids to see their grandparents, however, I decided to give it a shot.

On arriving at my father's compound on December 25, I knew coming to see him and others was one of the best decisions I had ever made; I still feel that way until this day.

In the village, my father had lost a great deal of weight due to old age. As I introduced my children to him that day, he began to shed tears. The women and neighbors in the village gathered and started to sing and dance with my mother for the safe return of my family and me. The sound of joy at my father's compound was ecstatic. Not saying much, I just held my father's hands. When I let go of his hands, he asked to hold each of my children's hands. It was extremely emotional and very memorable.

Determined to attend the Christmas Mass at my childhood Roman Catholic Church that day, I begged to leave and to return later to see him. From the church service, my family later returned to my father's compound. There were still many people gathered to welcome us, so I could not have as much of a conversation as I wanted to have with him. At night, when everyone had gone, I decided to spend some time with him, but he was asleep. The next day, many people gathered again and the excitement continued. At around four o'clock, my family began getting ready to go back to the city, Port-Harcourt, to catch our flights back to the United States that evening.

Nothing Left Undone

At that time, I said to myself, "There is no way I can go back to the United States without having an opportunity to chat with my father. Besides, I have no idea when I can visit him again." So, with people around or not, I determined to create time to converse with my father. And that's exactly what I did.

As my family gathered around him, there were several people surrounding him as usual. I gently asked that they excuse us, and they did. Then, I began to ask my father how he was feeling. After that discussion, I re-introduced my family to him, and while the kids placed their hands on his lap, I asked my father to bless them.

With a low voice, he responded, "Are the kids ready?"

"Yes, they are, Papa. Please speak louder, so we can hear you."

"I will, my daughter." Laughing, he joked, "You have seen how my voice has changed."

"You are fine, Papa. Just speak a bit louder."

When everyone was quiet, he started praying. "May God bless the children for me in Jesus' name," and we responded, "Amen."

"May the grace of our Lord Jesus Christ, the love of God, and the fellowship of the Holy Spirit, abide with you now and forever," and we replied, "Amen."

"Well, my children, whether it is good or bad, remember God. God is mighty. He does everything. If He does not

Perpetua Anaele

answer your prayer immediately, don't think He has left you. He is always with you. Now, behave well wherever you are or whatever you do. Don't disgrace me. I don't want to hear anything bad about you. Please remember God in whatever you are doing. May the grace of our Lord Jesus Christ, the love of God, and the fellowship of our Holy Spirit, abide with you now and forever," and we responded, "Amen."

After his prayer and advice, I thanked him and prayed for him as well. I then informed him that we would be returning to the United States, and that we would come back one day to see him. Asking him to stay well and to keep in touch, I kissed his forehead, hugged him, and told him goodbye.

"Remember me, Perpetua."

"Of course, I will always remember you, Papa. You are my father. Why wouldn't I?"

I then held his hands and began telling him how fortunate I was to be his daughter; how the upbringing he had given me had been very useful; and how grateful I was that he was there for me whenever I needed him. I also told him that I loved him very much, and that he was a great man. Adding that I was overjoyed to make him realize what he meant to me while he was still alive, I asked him to stay well. I kissed his forehead again and began to leave.

As I was leaving, my father continued to say, "Please remember me. Please remember me. Please remember me." As he kept saying this, my children became very emotional. I went back to him and told him that I would never forget him. I left the room tearfully, and that was the last time I saw my father.

Throughout that day in America, when I heard of his passing, I kept remembering the December 26, 2016 incident and thanking God that, at least, my family and I were able to see him for the last time that year. I also thanked God that I could let my father know in person how much I loved him for his tireless efforts in raising my siblings and me.

But dominating my thoughts that day was his last request to me: "Please remember me." I continued to ask myself if my father knew that he would be gone before I could see him again. If I had known that fact, I reasoned, I would never have gone back to the United States. I began to cry uncontrollably again.

Four weeks after my father's passing, my siblings and I in the United States, as well as our husbands, went to Nigeria to join the rest of the family to give him a well-deserved funeral.

Since his funeral, I had constantly contemplated the best way to remember my father as I promised. Suddenly, I had the thought of writing a book about his life and legacies. The goal being that I would not be the only one remembering him; so would his children, grandchildren, future generations, and the world alike. My idea of remembering my father in a profound way gave birth to this book. It is my hope that by sharing his life lessons with others, they, too, can perhaps learn from such lessons.

CHAPTER 3

HARD WORK DETERMINES SUCCESS

When I was about ten years old, my father relocated our family to a new compound, away from his extended family members. Our house in the new compound had ten bedrooms, was unfenced, and was surrounded by neighbors on both sides. It was located very close to the road, and at night, we could hear the sound of pedestrians passing by.

In the backyard, we had an open space where my sisters and I swept every morning. In front of the yard, my brother Pollycap—Bro. Polly—converted a portion of the yard to a flower garden. He planted different varieties, and when they began to bloom, their sweet fragrance attracted butterflies. In those days, young people in the community enjoyed spending most of their afternoons in our yard. They lauded Bro. Polly for his excellent landscaping skill. During sunny days, some would gather in front of our yard to either take nice photos with the colorful flowery background or simply hang out with others to enjoy the serenity of the environment.

Nothing Left Undone

On the left side of the yard was a large tangerine tree, which provided excellent shade for the family during sunny days; the tree also bore lots and lots of sweet tangerines every year. Most evenings, after completing the family chores, our family would sit under the tangerine tree, enjoying the breezy weather and telling jokes and stories.

My father epitomized hard work. Born in 1919 in Obite Etche, Rivers State, Nigeria, he was a handsome man from the depth of his dark eyes to the gentle expression of his voice. Reserved and tranquil, he was medium tall and a bit heavily built, with flawless brown skin. With a mix of gray and black hair on his scalp, my father had a perfectly inviting face that attracted people to him. He appeared well groomed at all times.

He grew up in a poverty-stricken family and faced various difficulties of the time. His parents—Mr. Nwaosuagwu of Umigbede, Obite Etche, and Ms. Nwaonuihe of Umuagbakolom, Umuoye Etche—neither went to school nor understood the value of education. He was the last born of the family, and none of his four siblings—Marcus, Paul, Nwafor, and Eligwe—went to school. He was also the last of his siblings to join his ancestors.

My father seemed to have many stories to tell; yet most times, he remained silent. I was probably fourteen years old when I first had a candid discussion with him. It was on a sunny Saturday afternoon, and he sat on his favorite black chair under the tangerine tree, enjoying beautiful blue sky and white clouds in windy weather. I stood behind him that afternoon, getting ready to remove some gray hair from his head. As I began massaging his head and removing the gray hair, I asked him to tell me what his childhood was like.

"Growing up was not easy, my daughter. I lost my mother at a very young age, and I was forced to become a man. With my two sisters married and gone to their husbands' homes, life became very difficult for me. On encountering this hardship, I realized then that I had two options—to accept the status quo and remain a prisoner of abject poverty for life, or to tackle the challenges head on, breaking the cycle of poverty. In those days, one had to decide what his or her destiny would be, and for me, I knew the only good option I had was to work hard against all odds to change my destiny for good.

"Over the years, I learned that every situation I faced was a lesson, and each challenge enabled me to grow as an individual. Without my mother to take care of me, I grew up to become a housekeeper, a fisherman, a farmer, a business man, and at the same time, a student. My day began before everyone else woke up and ended after everyone else went to bed. Each day, before going to school, I would sweep the compound, clean the house, prepare meals, and fetch water. Once I got home from school, I would rush to the farm to either plant cassava stems or harvest cassava tubers, fetch firewood, and set traps to kill animals for meat. At times, after arriving from the farm, I would rush to the stream to catch some fish."

"My goodness, Papa, with your family being poor, how were you able to survive financially?"

Nothing Left Undone

"It was not easy, my daughter. I often sold some meat and fish in the village, and using the proceeds, I supported my family." Smiling, he added, "It was a hobby I enjoyed very much, and one that taught me how to be responsible at a very young age. With time, , I learned to work in terms of knowing when to perform my household chores, as well as doing my homework."

"Papa, how were you able to travel from farm to stream, and to school? Were there means of transportation then?"

Raising and turning his head toward me, he asked, "Means of transportation? No way. Everybody in those days had to walk several miles to get to various places. I completed my farming, trapping, and selling chores by walking several miles a day. It was completely normal, and no one complained about it. As time went on, however, we had bicycles which helped make our lives better, and with the invention of motorcycles, we never had any reason to worry.

"Throughout those difficulties, I refused to be restricted by my family circumstances; instead, I learned different mechanisms to cope with my life. For example, I understood at a young age who I really was, and what I wanted to become in life. I also drew closer to God and became very involved in the Roman Catholic Church, which was the main church of my day. The suffering I experienced inspired me to become a teacher, mentoring others who were going through the same challenges as I was."

I was in awe of my father's dedication to give back to those around him.

"Did you have any friends, and if so, how did you relate to them, knowing that you were busy all the time?" I asked.

"Yes, I did have some friends, but as a young man who never had time to indulge in frivolities with my mates, I realized the importance of hard work. While my mates were busy getting married, having children, and becoming full-time farmers, I focused on my family's survival and my education; every other thing, such as getting married and having children, came later. In everything you do, my daughter, ensure you work hard, as hard work determines success."

Clearly, my father kept his eyes on the prize, and through hard work and determination, he pursued his ambition and became the only educated person in his parents' family. He was also the first person in his community—Obite Etche in Rivers State, Nigeria—to possess the First School Living Certificate, which is equivalent to a high school diploma in the United States. My father was the first person in his community to be admitted into college. Within Obite community, he was undeniably the first primary school teacher, and he encouraged others to follow suit.

In the Catholic Church parish in Etche, Rivers State, Nigeria, where he was a headmaster, the teachers referred to him as Manager's Torch, because he was often acting on behalf of the parish manager. Before the Nigerian Civil War broke out in 1967, my father was considered the father of all Etche teachers, and all the teachers lauded him for his hard work, his fatherly care toward them, and his passion for the teaching profession.

Nothing Left Undone

As a teacher, my father could read, speak, write, and understand English at an early age, becoming the first intermediary between the Obite community and the first white missionary Catholic priests who came to establish the community's Saint Mary's Catholic Church and School. He was dedicated to his duty as a missionary interpreter and represented the community and the priests to the best of his ability. Through his strong communication skill, he helped to resolve minor disputes that arose in establishing the church and the school and built trust between the community and the missionary priests.

My father's hard work virtue did not end there. He worked in various communities and cities in Nigeria, teaching and molding people's characters. At times, he was shuttling between Obite and the neighboring community where he was assigned; in other situations, he lived with his family at his assignment location.

Through his teaching career, he was posted to different communities, including at Saint Paul's ECN Amala in 1959, Saint Mary's RCM Azara Egbelu in 1960, Saint Anthony's RCM Ofekelem in 1961, Saint Joseph's Umuaturu in 1963, Saint John's Diobu in 1965, State School Umuoye in 1971, State School Elele in 1973, State School Nihi Etche in 1974, State School Ogida in 1976, State School Igbodo in 1978, State School Owu Etche in 1979, State School Obite Etche in 1980, State School Akpoku in 1984, and State School Ozuzu in 1990, where he honorably retired.

Perpetua Anaele

My Father- Third from the Left- With
Teachers at Azara Egbelu, 1960

My father recognized that it was not easy juggling his teaching career with raising a family, and he was, unquestionably, tired at times, but he never gave up. He was committed to his teaching profession and family and through hard work, he became disciplined and determined to succeed.

Mr. Lawrence Nwosu instilled in his children the virtues of hard work and determination. I remember one day when my father, Juliet, and I went to the farm to harvest some cassava tubers. In those days, the farms were located in remote areas, away from accessible roads. From the road, someone would transport the harvested cassava tubers either to the stream to be fermented or at home to be converted into garri. For this purpose, depending on the location of the farm, it could take about an hour for someone to carry a basket of cassava tubers from the farmland to the accessible road.

Nothing Left Undone

At the farm, my father ensured we had a division of labor in order to meet up with time. He would harvest the cassava tubers while Juliet and I carried the baskets of cassava to the accessible road. Because there were many of us in my family, my father would harvest enough to make at least five bags of garri or cassava flour. That meant that Juliet and I would go many times—as many as six—to transport the cassava tubers to the accessible road. While we did that, the cassava transporter would carry the harvested cassava tubers on his motorcycle to the house, where the rest of the family members would begin the garri processing.

The garri process in those days included hand peeling and washing the cassava tubers, machine grinding the tubers, bagging the ground cassava, tying the bags with sticks, and setting aside the bags for three days to dry.

On the third day, my sisters would untie the cassava bags, sieve the cassava, and begin the ritual of frying the cassava into garri. At times, the frying process would take two people all day to complete. The garri would then be allowed to cool off, be bagged, and later be sold at the local market for the family upkeep.

While some of my family members would process garri, others would walk down to the stream to begin the process of producing cassava flour. At the stream, they would pour the transported cassava tubers into a designated portion of the stream, leaving them there for four to five days to ferment. Once the cassava tubers were fermented, my sisters would return to the stream, peel the fermented cassava tubers, and sieve and bag them. They would then dry the bagged cassava by mechanically pressing out water from the bag and transporting them to the local market, where they would be sold as cassava flour. Depending on the quantity of cassava tubers, two people could spend all day at the stream, processing them into flour. The task was not easy, but we could not survive on our parents' meager teaching salaries alone, because at times, they would not be paid for three to four months.

As children, our father taught us to work hard in whatever we did. Through his popular slogan, *suffer before pleasure*, he passed on many great life lessons to us, using his life as a case study. He displayed to us why hard work can change a bad situation into good, improving our lives. He was an accomplished and a contented man despite the fact that he was not rich.

Through my father's success story, I am constantly reminded that hard work pays off. In the same way that he worked hard in life to transition from nothing to something, I am reminded that someone who does not work hard in life can become a total failure, irrespective of how rich his or her parents are or were.

Biblically, Jesus recognizes the importance of hard work. In His Parable of the Lost Son, Jesus describes a situation where a man had two sons; the younger son asked his father to give him his share of the family property. His father gave him his property as he requested. Instead of investing that property and working hard to make more profit, the son gathered all of his belongings, including the money and the property, and departed to a distant land. On arriving there,

Nothing Left Undone

he squandered his wealth by living flamboyantly. After he had spent all he had, there was a famine in that land, and he began to be in need. No one could help him. The situation was so dire that he had to find a job taking care of pigs in the field. He desired to feed off of the pods that the pigs were eating, but no one wanted to give him anything. He later came to his senses, returned to his father, and asked for his forgiveness. His father immediately forgave him and celebrated his return (Luke 15:11–32).

Although the emphasis of Jesus' parable of the Lost Son is on the need for us to forgive one another, it also shows that whatever we are given, we need to work hard and make good use of it. If the lost son had made good use of his property and had become more successful than his father, there would not have been a need for him to ask his father for forgiveness. In fact, his father would have been more delighted to have such a hardworking and an illustrious son.

In addition, the Parable of the Talents in Matthew 25:14–30 is a reminder that we must wisely invest the talents God has given us. Here, Jesus talks about a man who was going on a journey, but before he did, he entrusted his wealth to his three servants according to their abilities. To one, he gave five bags of gold; to another he gave two bags of gold; and to the last one, he gave one bag of gold.

When he left for his journey, the servants began to do something with the gold he had given them. The man with the five bags of gold put them to work and gained five additional bags of gold in the process; the one with the two bags of gold did the same thing and gained two additional bags of gold in return; but the man with only one bag of gold simply dug a hole and buried it.

After a long time, their master returned and contacted them to settle his accounts with them. The man, who had received five bags of gold came with the additional five bags of gold, saying, "Master, you entrusted me with five bags of gold. See, I have gained five more" (Matthew 25:20).

The master, very excited, responded, "Well done, good and faithful servant! You have been faithful with a few things; I will put you in charge of many things. Come and share your master's happiness!" (v. 21).

The man with two bags of gold also came, saying to his master, "You entrusted me with two bags of gold; see, I have gained two more" (v. 22).

The master, very pleased with him, also said, "Well done, good and faithful servant! You have been faithful with a few things; I will put you in charge of many things. Come and share your master's happiness!" (v. 23).

Then came the man with only one bag of gold, saying to his master, "I knew that you are a hard man, harvesting where you have not sown and gathering where you have not scattered seed. So I was afraid and went out and hid your gold in the ground. See, here is what belongs to you" (vs. 24–25).

Nothing Left Undone

His master, being very furious, said to him,

> "You wicked, lazy servant! So you knew that I harvest where I have not sown and gather where I have not scattered seed? Well then, you should have put my money on deposit with the bankers, so that when I returned, I would have received it back with interest. So take the bag of gold from him and give it to the one who has ten bags. For whoever has will be given more, and they will have an abundance. Whoever does not have, even what they have will be taken from them. And throw that worthless servant outside, into the darkness, where there will be weeping and gnashing of teeth" (Matthew 25:26–30).

The story is an interesting illustration of why hard work pays off. Someone might argue that it was not fair to the man who had only one bag of gold to have his gold taken from him and given to the man who already had ten. On the contrary, such an argument is unfounded. The man with one talent did not invest wisely. Even if he did not want to work hard, he could have invested the money in the bank to yield interest for the master, but he chose not to. So, no matter how many times his master allows him to work with the bag of gold, he will definitely not be successful. It is, therefore, beneficial for the master to give the bag of gold to someone who would manage it better. With now eleven bags of gold, the first man could double them, gaining twenty-two bags of gold for the master.

The bottom line is that Jesus wants us to work hard. Even God, who created us wonderfully with unique characteristics and talents, works hard. When we were introduced to Him in Genesis, He was already working until the seventh day when He rested. Since He created us in His image, He does not expect us to sit at home without being productive. It does not please Him if we simply do not use the talents He has given us and then turn around to blame Him for our misfortunes. He wants us to discover our talents and put them into action.

Over the years, I have relied heavily on my father's hard work advice to succeed in life. At times, I contacted him when I faced life challenges that tried my patience. During those challenging times, he reminded me of the importance of hard work and joked that it is not supposed to be easy; that's why it is called hard work.

An example of when my father's advice was useful to me was in 1995. Shortly after I arrived in the United States in 1994, I began to face a culture shock. At that time, I found it slightly challenging adjusting to the new environment.

The temperature in Maryland that winter was too cold, and I kept wondering how people were able to go to school and work during such a cold temperature. In addition, I wanted to go to an open market to buy some fresh African food but could not find any. It was also not easy for me to make friends, as most people I met were either speaking too

Nothing Left Undone

fast that I could not understand them, or they, too, could not understand me because of my accent. I began to miss my family and friends so dearly and longed to see them. As a result, I continuously contemplated abandoning my education and life in America to return to Nigeria, my then comfort zone.

Then, I remembered my father's hard work legacy and reflected on what he would have advised me to do to overcome my culture shock. I knew he would have encouraged me to remain in America and pursue my dreams; he would have advised that if I worked hard enough and kept my eyes on the prize, I would achieve my dreams and reap the reward of my hard work. My father would also have encouraged me to avoid stressing myself on things I did not have control over. After thinking these through, I decided to stay in America and work hard to achieve my dreams. As I did, I attained my goals in no time. Today, with the support of my husband, I have also instilled this virtue in my children.

In addition, being in the United States Foreign Service, my family and I have lived and worked in five countries—Bangladesh, Ghana, Mozambique, Rwanda, and Senegal. Through my Foreign Service experience, I have come to realize and appreciate what it is like as a young parent, as my father was, to raise children while traveling and working. Such an endeavor, undoubtedly, requires dedication and endurance, and I am grateful that I have learned such lessons from my father.

It is my hope that everyone can learn and appreciate the importance of my father's legacy of hard work, because for us humans, there will always be challenges. They are a part of our existence. Challenges may come in the form of lost loved ones or lost breadwinners, bankruptcy, divorce, unemployment, illnesses, or another unanticipated development. The recent coronavirus is an example of such an unforeseen circumstance. Our ability to work our way back up through hard work and perseverance will determine if we can survive as individuals. We must realize that such challenges are not always bad for us, nor are they signs of rejection from God. If we learn from our challenges, work hard, and have faith in God, we will come out better than we were and be ready to help others.

My father rewrote his history and achieved his goals in life. We, too, can do the same, if not more, by learning to work hard and be determined to succeed. He always advised us- his children- to dream to become someone important and to work hard to actualize our dreams. My father warned that in life, there will always be setbacks, but that we should never allow such setbacks to derail us. He added that we should not give up even in difficult situations and not be afraid to make mistakes. He suggested that as we keep working hard and pursuing our dreams, one day, we will succeed. Knowing these, therefore, we should work hard in life, never be afraid to make mistakes, learn from our mistakes, and use the lessons from our mistakes to improve our lives.

CHAPTER 4

EDUCATION IS PRICELESS

Education is the most powerful weapon which you can use to change the world.
— **Nelson Mandela**

One sunny and humid Friday evening, my father sat on his chair in the backyard, fanning and cooling down himself with an old newspaper in his right hand. With his left hand, he was eating a well roasted corn on the cob my mother had just prepared for him. In front of him was a small center table with a bowl of two roasted pieces of corn. I slowly walked toward my father, asking if I could get him some water to drink.

"Yes, please," he responded.

I brought the water, handed it to him, and started walking away.

"Perpetua," he called, "grab a chair and come and sit near me."

Perpetua Anaele

I did as he had instructed. Pointing to the bowl of corn while looking at me, he said, "Help yourself."

"No, Papa, I'm fine."

"Come on, don't be shy. I know you want some corn, so go for it," he insisted.

He was actually right that I wanted some, so I took one and began to eat slowly.

"How was school today, my daughter?"

"Long and boring as usual, Papa."

There was silence as we both continued to chew our corn.

"Did you feel the same way when you were growing up?" I asked, breaking the silence.

"No, my daughter. During my time, I did not have any choice. I lived through perhaps the most difficult period of time. Many people never went to school and those who did, did so at an old age. Social amenities were completely nonexistent. For example, the road was either absent or ruined, and many communities did not have schools. I had to walk several miles on bumpy, unpaved roads to attend a missionary-supported elementary school in another community. There was also no good means of transportation, which meant that I had to walk several miles to attend my classes. Since the roads were poor, there were at times snakes and other dangerous animals along the way. I had

Nothing Left Undone

to consciously protect myself to avoid being bitten by such animals.

"In those days too, there was no electricity, and the main sources of light at night were lamps and firewood; this meant that I had to complete my homework on time, or I would be unable to catch up the next day. No water at home also meant that I had to walk multiple miles to the stream to fetch some; otherwise, the family would not have any to drink, cook, clean, or take showers. Moreover, there was no hospital in the community, which meant that if I became sick, I would have to either use a local concoction to cure myself, wait without any medication to get better, or travel to the city, which was several miles away, to seek care. Despite the challenges, I never gave up on education, because it is priceless."

Stunned with the level of challenges my father went through, I reacted by saying, "That's crazy, Papa. What a difficult way to live! I'm glad I was not born then."

"This is why I don't understand it when you complain that your school is long and boring, my daughter. You have everything in life to succeed academically, so you have no reason to complain whatsoever. At least, you have a school in this community, and life is not too bad compared to my time. So, next time I ask you how school is, tell me it is great. Is that clear?"

Without looking at him, I responded, "Yes, Papa. Thank you."

On noticing that I was uncomfortable with the conversation, he suggested, "You can leave now if you want."

I quickly got up and left as fast as I could, feeling that he was unsympathetic to my situation. Although I was a bit uneasy with my father's lecture on the importance of education, I never forgot the look on his face that day. The discussion proved to me that if he could survive such challenges and attain his educational goal, I, too, could do it better than he did.

Admittedly, my father was an outstanding educator who had foresight about the power of education to change an individual, a family, a community, and a nation. At a time when his mates were focused on farming and raising families, he saw the potential in education and pursued it tenaciously.

He first determined his purpose in life, which was to set himself apart from his peers through school, and then he outlined a road map to achieving that purpose. In following through with his plans to achieve his dream, he neither wavered nor gave up.

A review of his educational records showed that he acquired his First School Living Certificate from Saint Francis in Obike, Imo State, in 1954. After obtaining this certificate, he later went back to school to garner his Grade III Teachers' Certificate in 1958 from the then Eastern Region Ministry of Education in eastern Nigeria. This certificate was a benchmark for teaching in those days.

He began teaching in 1959 and later went back to school to earn his Grade II Teachers' Certificate from Saint John's College in Diobu, Port-Harcourt, Rivers State, in 1966. In

Nothing Left Undone

June 1983, my father received his Associate Certificate in Education (ACE) from the University of Ibadan in Oyo, Western Nigeria. Through his love for education, he made the groundbreaking achievement of becoming the first teacher in his community.

My Father, an ACE Graduate, University of Ibadan, 1983

Casting my mind back across the years, I have a glimpse of how the people in my father's days were living. Not having a hospital in his community in the mid-1900s does not surprise me at all because, as of 2021, there is still no hospital in the same community. I have heard of people, such as pregnant women and accident victims, dying, because the nearest hospital was too far; therefore, they could not get there in time to be given care.

Besides the lack of social amenities, people in those days also lacked role models, who could encourage them to get educated. My father saw the world transform from absence of social amenities and knowledge to a period of increase in social amenities, knowledge, and technological know-how. These changes shaped him into who he was. Despite these challenges and changes, he persevered and pursued education no matter what.

As I grew older, I began to recognize and appreciate the sacrifices my father and others in his time had made to become who they were. I wondered what it was like growing up without cell phones, the Internet, or televisions. As my father rightly pointed out years ago, my generation has been given everything on a platter of gold—we have the Internet, computers, talented teachers, and schools in every community.

I remember when I was growing up and my father bought his first television. Every evening, he would display the TV in the middle of his compound while villagers gathered to watch it until midnight. The only channel we had then was a news channel, which was in black and white pictures.

My generation also has great means of transportation, electricity, borehole water, and other social amenities. Therefore, there is no reason we should not seek one of the greatest things in our lives, education; there is no justification whatsoever.

Sadly, however, as an adult, I have seen some families who refuse to invest academically in their children. They forget to realize that they are depriving their children an important source of survival in this modern world—education.

Some families continue to depend solely on land as their main source of survival. They don't recognize that land is fixed and cannot be expanded. This means that for a family of five who depended on ten plots of land many decades ago, today, such a family is, unquestionably, doubled in size and may not survive on the same expanse. In addition, the constant farming on the same piece of land year after year depletes the nutrients in the soil. This explains why certain families continue to fight during farming seasons in Nigeria.

While it is true that some of these people may open up businesses instead of going to school, from my experience, I have noticed that an individual with a degree can manage a business better than an individual without one. If a family member, for example, were to be educated, that individual could find a high paying job in the city and support his or her family. Likewise, the individual could purchase his or her own piece of land, instead of depending on the family land. Such an act would make land available to those in the family who must depend on it to survive.

Perpetua Anaele

Educated people also ensure that their children are educated, and the trend continues in their generations given the rippling effect of education. Such an endeavor will prevent the circle of poverty. The beauty of education is that it opens doors for and equalizes people: if someone has a degree in a village, that person can compete favorably with another who has a degree in the city. Education humbles an individual, positioning the person's mind to think differently and achieve more. Every successful educated individual is celebrated wherever he or she is. This is why I cannot applaud my father enough for being so visionary as to pursue education not only for himself but for his entire family.

My educational life is, indeed, a success story. I grew up the fifth of nine children in a nuclear family. My parents had ten children—six females and four males. Unfortunately, one of my brothers, Vanacious, passed away at the age of six. Currently, nine of us alive are educated. It was not easy for my father to raise his children, especially my sisters and me.

In my primary school years, life was hard, and opportunities for women were limited. If a woman had a female child, it was considered that she did not have any child at all. She would be ridiculed for having a female child. Only male children were celebrated.

Now, consider that during my father's time, many men were into polygamy in order to have many children who could assist them with farming. In spite of the pressure from his colleagues to forget about education and focus on polygamy and farming, my father never saw the need to do so. In addition, when he finally got married and my mother began

Nothing Left Undone

to have mainly female children, the external pressure on him to marry another woman became worse. Think for a second what my parents must have gone through in those days.

Some years ago, my mother told me an interesting story of her childbearing years. "If a woman had a male child, people would gather and give the child a name. There was always a great celebration. If she gave birth to a female child, however, she was on her own. Due to the number of girls I had, people were predicting the outcome of my next pregnancy. After I gave birth to a girl, only a few would celebrate with my family," she narrated.

My mother commented that she would hear some people encouraging my father to marry another woman who could give him male children. Others would laugh and say they would never go to my mother's village to marry, as women from her community only give birth to female children.

While growing up, too, I faced the societal realization that a woman's education was expected to start and end in the kitchen. Given that limited educational opportunities were available for women, I was ridiculed when I began going to school. I remember an encounter I had with a man in the community when I was walking down to school one day. He said to me, "Why are you wasting your time every day going to school? I cannot believe your father is foolish enough to be wasting his hard-earned income to train you, a female. Anyway, by the time, you are trained and a man comes and marries you, your father will have realized how stupid he has been."

Perpetua Anaele

As a child, I never realized that he was wrong. I came home from school that day, crying and complaining to my father about the incident. My father, however, told me that if he was a fool for sending his female children to school, he was more than happy to be one. He reaffirmed Aristotle's belief, "The roots of education are bitter, but the fruit is sweet," encouraging me to develop a passion for learning, and that the sky would be my limit. Using himself as a case study, my father explained to me that education was a tool to set me free and change my life from bad to good. While enlightening me on the importance of education as a woman, he made me realize that I was somebody, but I could be a better person with education. My father added that the best investment anyone can pursue is education, as it is priceless.

After my discussion with my father, I never responded or paid attention to that man whenever he confronted me. Looking back years ago, I do not blame him. He was, in fact, emphasizing what was normal because in those days, girls were not allowed to have their voices heard; they were trained to be stay-at-home mothers, capable only of caring for their husbands and children.

Today, I consider myself and my sisters lucky. We are lucky because while our society undervalued females then, our father did the exact opposite. We are lucky because our father, being a headmaster, saw the potential in investing in education not only for his male children but also for his female children. We are lucky, because our father was visionary enough to realize very early that when a girl or a woman is educated, her family, community, and nation benefit. And we are lucky, because our father gave us the tool—education—to succeed. My five sisters and I took advantage of the opportunity our father presented us and went to school by all means. Consequently, today, we are all educated by the grace of God. We are also employed and are contributing positively to our respective societies.

In July 2020, while unpacking my family boxes that were in my garage, I coincidentally saw an open envelope that was addressed to Perpetua Nwosu. I anxiously looked at the content of the envelope and saw letters that my father had written me years ago. In one of the letters dated August 6, 2000, he wrote,

"Dearly beloved daughter,

In the first place, I ought to ask about your present condition of health together with your children and husband. I hope you are taking your studies seriously. I know you will not play with your studies. Try to work hard because of the condition of things nowadays. As for us, we are not doing badly…"

After reading the letters and reflecting on the encouraging words from my father, I broke down, crying at his passing but thanked God for giving me such an intelligent and a decent father.

Not many females of my time were as lucky as my siblings and I were. They faced different obstacles, which made it difficult for them to finish or even start school. Some of these challenges included a lack of resources, gender inequality, and the constraints of domestic violence. Due to harsh corporal punishments at school and succumbing to the societal ideology that "a woman's education ends in the kitchen," some of my female classmates dropped out of school. They became focused in farming, raising money for their brothers to receive education instead. Some got married and began having children at very early ages. Today, I think about those girls who did not have the educational advantage that I had. I also think about those girls who continue to be deprived of basic education. Across the world, young women and girls continue to face barriers to education.

Investing in female education is one of the most important things a nation can do. When a woman is educated, she takes better care of her home, raising her children better, and contributing positively to the building of her nation.

Recognizing the importance of female education, therefore, every nation should give its women and girls educational, leadership, and business skill opportunities, so they can secure their livelihoods. Doing so can help lift them from poverty and reduce maternal and child mortalities. Everyone needs to be an active participant in the task to educate women and girls. People in leadership should use their platforms to teach girls life skills and values that can help them to succeed. Every nation should engage in dialogues with women in leadership positions who can inspire girls and women to dream big and succeed. We must make way for the next generation of female leaders through providing

Nothing Left Undone

our girls and women a quality education. Educated girls and children should be encouraged to go into public service and make the world a better place for all. Boys and men should also be empowered to promote gender equality.

Years ago, when I was in primary school, a female pupil, Charity, normally sat behind me in class. She hardly participated in class, but one day, our English teacher asked the class, "Who can make a sentence with a monkey?"

Surprisingly, Charity raised her hand in readiness to answer the question. The teacher then asked her to stand up and answer the question. With much confidence, Charity shouted, "I am a monkey."

The class began to laugh, and the teacher turned to her and said, "Did you just say you are a monkey?"

She responded, "I am a monkey."

Instead of encouraging her for standing up for the first time to answer a question and asking the class to stop laughing, the teacher said, "Class, you have heard Charity. From today, call her a monkey."

They all continued to laugh, shouting and calling her a monkey. As the pupils returned home from school that day, they publicized the incident within the community. Consequently, everyone at home was calling Charity a monkey. She began to cry, and throughout our primary school years, she never volunteered to answer any other question. She managed to complete her high school education, and that was it; Charity never furthered her education, partly due to the embarrassment she had received while in primary school.

Thus, when we look for role models for girls, that teacher, obviously, is not the type of person we are looking for, as he ruined Charity's educational prospects. We need people who can see the potential in girls beyond their mistakes. We need role models or mentors who can encourage girls to be bold and express their minds. There is nothing wrong with a girl who is confident enough to pursue an ambitious undertaking. That should be our message as we empower girls to be the best they can be. When women and girls are empowered, they realize their value in society and assist in sustaining economies, creating a more prosperous world.

No doubt, many women have succeeded academically. Such women should become advocates for struggling girls, highlighting to these young women that every obstacle can be surmounted. Every woman should enjoy freedom, equity, and inclusiveness in world's affairs. Civil society organizations should advance the status of women and girls in every society.

My father's zeal to pursue education for himself and his children did not end there. He married my mother when she was in secondary school. Due to his passion for education, he assisted her to further her education. This is very remarkable, because an average man would not have bothered to advance his wife's education.

Nothing Left Undone

When I was growing up, my parents were both teachers, bringing in two separate incomes, although small, to support the family. When my father retired from teaching, my mother continued to support the family through teaching until she, too, later retired.

My father also encouraged many people in his community to be educated. During his funeral in 2017, we—his family—received amazing eulogies from people whose lives he helped change.

My father lived to help people and knew that as individuals, we all have the potential for greatness, and that the goal for achieving that greatness is through education. No wonder a popular African American slogan says, "A mind is a terrible thing to waste but a wonderful thing to invest in."

Through education, people can become a force for change in their communities. They can invest in social changes and better the future. Think of world leaders who have helped shape the world by bringing about social justices. What they share in common is that they were or are educated. Mahatma Gandhi, for example, was an Indian lawyer who was instrumental in the Indian freedom struggle against its colonial masters. Through his nonviolent civil protests, he successfully led his country to independence in 1947. He could not have been successful without education.

This is also true for President Barack Obama. On January 20, 2009, he became the first African American president of the United States of America. His popular "Yes, we can" slogan and passion for education enabled him to pursue his dream of becoming the first African American president. A lawyer by training, President Obama is confident that he can be whoever he wants to be. His unwavering belief in success could not have been possible without his education.

How about Kamala Harris? Ms. Harris was born in Oakland, California, on October 20, 1964 by an Indian mother and a Jamaican father. She was only 7 years old when her parents were divorced. Her mother, a PhD holder, raised her and her sister in California, inculcating in them the importance of a good education. Despite the challenges of growing up in a single parent household, Ms. Harris worked so hard and became a lawyer and politician. She occupied very important positions, including a county district court attorney, an attorney general of California, and a senator. On January 20, 2021, Ms. Kamala Harris became the first female African American and first Indian American vice president of the United States of America. This position made her the highest-ranking female elected official in the history of the United States of America. Without being educated, there is no way she could have achieved these milestones in her life.

My father left the legacy that education is priceless. He knew that education is key to a successful life. He took his time to become educated and in turn, invested in his family's education, encouraging others in society to do the same. Today, his children are fulfilling his legacy, and by the grace of God, this legacy will continue.

If you do not believe in the importance of education, take me as an example. There is no way I could have written this book without being educated. My father gave me the tool I needed to function globally as an individual. His mentoring me to be educated has enabled me to help my family, my community, and my nation. Through my education, and with a support from my husband, I have inspired my children to be their best, and they are doing the same. I have contributed to assisting my community by working with my husband to inspire others to seek all that education can offer.

I have also joined my husband to carry out diplomatic assignments for the United States in five embassies across the world. I could not have successfully done it without being educated. If I can do it, others could do it even better than me.

Education being priceless is a tremendous legacy that my father left, and I am hoping that others, too, can embrace the legacy. Education is worth it, because it requires us to grow, and as the saying goes, we stop growing the moment we stop learning.

CHAPTER 5

DARE TO LEAD

My father, in an effort to dare me to lead, called me to his living room on Christmas Eve of 1993. As I entered the room, he said, pointing to elegantly wrapped gifts on the table, "These are for me from two of our illustrious sons abroad."

Excited about what the gifts were, I quickly walked closer to the presents and responded, "Really? What are they, and who are the illustrious sons, Papa?"

"You can open the packages and see for yourself, my daughter."

Enthusiastically, I unwrapped the packages and found two beautiful Christmas greeting cards and two foreign-made sweaters for men. Lifting up the gifts, I said, "Wow, these are nice, Papa."

"Undoubtedly, my daughter. You can read the notes on the cards." I did so slowly, looking at my father as I read to monitor his reaction to the emotional words on the cards.

He sat down, smiling as I continued to read and laugh with joy.

Raising my voice, I asked, "What did you do for these men, Papa, to merit this type of generosity?"

"My daughter, you know that every Christmas, I receive gifts from our sons abroad. Years ago, I taught them in primary school and encouraged them to pursue their dreams without fear. I had a premonition that they would succeed and knew that every child was important. They followed my advice and from time to time, they contacted me for more advice, and I never hesitated in helping them. Today, they have succeeded and have never forgotten me. Even if they do not visit Nigeria often, they somehow send me some gifts in appreciation for what I did for them. I feel I don't deserve their generosity, but they keep doing this year after year. I guess it only means one thing—in life, we need to dare to lead by encouraging others to succeed."

"Lucky you, Papa. It does, indeed, pay to be a leader."

Being goal-oriented is an important attribute of a great leader. When you are goal-oriented, you have a clear mandate, and you can work toward achieving that mandate no matter what. Such a person will most likely encounter some difficulties along the way but will be resilient, remaining focused and positive until the goal is achieved. He or she thinks strategically, plans intelligently, and communicates skillfully. With intense focus, a goal-oriented person takes great risks and attracts others to him or herself due to the purpose-driven characteristics the person possesses.

Perpetua Anaele

You cannot be a leader if you do not know the way and lead others in the right direction. If you consider yourself a leader but do not know the way, your followers will, indisputably, get lost. A leader is not always right but depends on his or her followers to solve some problems. To do so, he or she has to be a good listener and be willing to coordinate with his or her followers to achieve a goal.

Due to the unique characteristics of a leader, not everyone is a great leader. In our earthly standard, a great leader possesses the following characteristics: honesty and integrity, ability to inspire others, commitment and passion, decision making capability, delegation capacity, accountability, creativity, communication skills, and related attributes. A great leader must set a standard for others to follow. You cannot ask someone to be honest when you are not; you must lead by example.

Nelson Mandela was a great leader. He got tired of the way his people in South Africa were being treated, and he decided to become a lawyer in order to help them fight their social injustices. After becoming a lawyer, he began speaking out against social injustices, the apartheid system, in South Africa. Among his people, he commanded respect and modeled humility. Even when he was imprisoned, he endured much suffering but kept his eyes on the prize.

After spending twenty-seven years in prison, he was released, and he became the first black South African president. Surprisingly, using the notion of reconciliation, he re-united all South Africans, black and white, handling the issues of his day by persuasion and not by force. Mr. Mandela showed

Nothing Left Undone

his oppressors kindness when he could have retaliated based on what they did to him and his people. Selflessly, when it was time for him to hand over power, he did so willingly. After his retirement from public service, he continued his involvement in programs that targeted the eradication of poverty in the world.

In his famous speech in London in 2005, "Make Poverty History," he demonstrated his strong leadership qualities. He brilliantly said in his speech that poverty is not natural, just as slavery and apartheid are not. He added that they are man-made and can be eliminated by human beings. Nelson Mandela encouraged people to work toward eradicating poverty, commenting that in as much as poverty still remains with us, we cannot be free. He was absolutely right.

Nelson Mandela was one man whose actions changed the lives of many. He united many people to love and respect one another and to live in peace. He turned South African hope into action and left a legacy of making sure that people's lives are fundamentally changed. Although Mandela died in 2013, his legacy still lives on.

Dr. Martin Luther King, Jr. was another great leader. Born on January 15, 1929 to a Baptist pastor, Dr. King became educated and continued his family's pastoral lineage. Like Nelson Mandela, Dr. King became tired of the suffering he and his fellow black people were going through in America, and he decided to use his pastoral skill to change the status quo. Applying his nonviolence demonstration campaign, he led the civil rights movement and brought about beneficial changes for his people. He was arrested about thirty times and faced public humiliation in the process.

In one of his peaceful demonstrations, he attracted 250,000 people in Washington, D.C., delivering his famous "I Have a Dream" speech. Sadly, while standing at the balcony of his motel room in Memphis, Tennessee, on April 4, 1968, waiting to continue a nonviolent demonstration on behalf of the city's garbage collectors, he was assassinated. Today, the United States of America honors Dr. King by celebrating his birthday on the third Monday of January as a federal holiday.

Another great leader was Abraham Lincoln, one of the presidents of the United States of America. During his time, the country owned slaves, but he stood up boldly for what he believed in, emancipating slaves and preserving the Union in America. Although he was assassinated on April 14, 1865, his legacy still remains.

George Washington, the American Founding Father, was also a great leader. Through his extraordinary leadership qualities, he successfully led the American Revolution, becoming the first president of the country.

Biblically, the definition of a great leader slightly defers from the worldly definition. In the letter of Saint Paul to Titus, Paul describes an elder or a leader as one who is "blameless, faithful to his wife, a man whose children believe and are not open to the charge of being wild and disobedient" (Titus 1:6).

He also adds that the elder must not be "overbearing, not quick-tempered, not given to drunkenness, not violent, not pursuing dishonest gain. Rather, he must be hospitable, one who loves what is good, who is self-controlled, upright, holy and disciplined" (Titus 1:7–8).

Some examples of biblical characters who portrayed great leadership qualities were Moses and Joshua. The Bible gives detailed accounts of the challenges those two great leaders went through. Under the guidance of God, for example, Moses led the Israelites from Egypt to the wilderness. During this exodus, the Israelites grumbled about one issue or another, time and time again, testing Moses' patience. They questioned why God did not allow them to remain in Egypt instead of bringing them to the wilderness to die. The Israelites soon forgot the anguish that they were going through in Egypt, and some even preferred to go back there. Despite the challenges, Moses still led them to the wilderness.

After the death of Moses, Joshua took over and led the Israelites to the Promised Land. He, too, underwent various challenges but never lost focus, and in the end, he overcame them.

In Luke 9:46–50, Jesus' disciples argue over who among them is the greatest. Jesus takes a little child and tells them that whoever welcomes a little child, welcomes Him and that the least among them is the greatest. The greatest person must descend from his or her high horse and be willing to be submissive. Titles and positions do not matter to God. Just as Jesus left all of His heavenly glory and came to this world to save us, a great leader must be willing to serve others and not to be served.

Living a humble life, Jesus was born poor in a stable and never displayed His richness; He humbled Himself to wash the feet of His disciples, ate with unbelievers, and died a shameful death on the cross, just to save us. Today, His heavenly Father has recognized Him, giving Him the name above all other names "that at the name of Jesus, every knee should bow, in heaven and on earth and under the earth, and every tongue acknowledge that Jesus Christ is Lord, to the glory of God, the Father" (Philippians 2:10–11).

In 1 Peter, 5:1-4, Peter says, "To the elders among you, I appeal as a fellow elder and a witness of Christ's sufferings who also will share in the glory to be revealed. Be shepherds of God's flock that is under your care, watching over them—not because you must, but because you are willing, as God wants you to be; not pursuing dishonest gain, but eager to serve; not lording it over those entrusted to you, but being examples to the flock; And when the Chief Shepherd appears, you will receive the crown of glory that will never fade away."

Peter is clearly asking the leaders to take care of people entrusted to them. Today, however, I have seen some leaders who abuse the people under their care. Instead of taking care of the people assigned to them, they take from them. Some leaders are into leadership for what they can gain from it. They go into leadership as poor, but a few months later, they become millionaires. Instead of mentoring the people who are under their care, these leaders harass them. In spite

Nothing Left Undone

of being asked to lead their people to greener pastures, they lead them to barren land. They forget their duty as shepherds: their flock should not be in need of anything. Some leaders, despite how old and incapable of leading they are, remain in power to the detriment of their followers.

Based on the biblical and worldly descriptions of a great leader, Mr. Lawrence Nwalozie Nwosu was such a person. He lived an impeccable life, worthy of emulation. His life was characterized by the ideology of "self last and others first." He inspired people to dream big and achieve those dreams.

When he was young, he had a vision that the only way to be different from others was to be educated. Detailing his life's mission statement, he brilliantly outlined his goals and ensured that they were attainable. Since one of his mission statements was to become a teacher, he envisioned himself working in the teaching profession and set a roadmap to getting there. My father knew he had to like what he wanted to be in order to be a happy man. He could have chosen a medical career, for instance, but he chose teaching, because he felt that would complete him.

Applying the characteristics of a leader, such as resilience, strategic thinking, empathy, enthusiasm, intelligence, courageous, as well as organizational and communication skills, Mr. Nwosu achieved his goal of becoming a teacher. Then, he toured various communities in Nigeria to teach and mold the lives of others. He also encouraged many in these communities to become teachers, increasing the

Perpetua Anaele

number of capable teachers in Nigeria. He taught by example, motivating others to follow his footsteps.

Through education, my father changed the trajectory of those around him from poverty to wealth. Consequently, he received the reward of living an accomplished life and seeing firsthand the positive impact of lives he had been able to touch. Many of those he inspired to become great teachers, achieved more than he did in the profession. This is a remarkable quality of a great leader as indicated by John Quincy Adams: "If your actions inspire others to dream more, learn more, do more, and become more, you are a leader."

In line with his roadmap to success, Mr. Nwosu knew when he wanted to get married and the type of family he wished to have. While his male counterparts were busy getting many wives, he never wavered from his original plan or compared himself to them. Instead, he was married to only one woman and raised a great family.

As a compassionate leader, my father took responsibility of those under his care. Years ago, when I was attending a secondary school in Obite community, some schoolteachers were living in my father's house while working at the school. Because they came from faraway places, they relied on my father as their mentor. He protected them in the community and handled their issues, as if they were his own.

Once, one of the teachers impregnated a girl who lived in the village. The girl's family was angry with the teacher, because he had impregnated their daughter out of wedlock and never

Nothing Left Undone

intended to marry her. Given that impregnating a young woman out of wedlock was considered a taboo, the girl's family members threatened to harm the teacher for violating their daughter. It was a very serious issue. My father, being respected in the community, met with the elders of the community and the family of the girl, apologizing and promising that the teacher would take care of the girl until she gave birth. Out of respect for my father, the community accepted, and said it would hold my father responsible if things did not go well.

During the girl's pregnancy, my father was involved to ensure that nothing bad happened to her. In the process, he realized that the girl had refused to comply with the terms of agreement, such as attending her antenatal visits. He helped the teacher bring the matter up to the family of the girl. Everyone, including the family of the girl, tried to persuade her to seek medical care but for some reason, she refused to do so. Sadly, she and her baby passed away during childbirth. This became an additional issue, as the community was threatening to deal with the teacher.

My father then met with the community again and was able to calm everyone down. The issue was later resolved amicably as the family of the girl blamed her for not taking care of herself. The teacher was so pleased with my father that throughout the time he spent teaching in the community school, he never forgot what my father did for him. It was such a peaceful ending that the teacher married a woman in the same community before the end of his teaching assignment there.

Perpetua Anaele

As a true leader, my father's integrity was never in question. He was genuine, and many people relied on him for his honesty. Many years ago, he was a headmaster and was entrusted with teachers' salaries. Every month, when the Schools' Board, an office that handled the management of school programs in Nigeria, allocated him teachers' salaries to pay the teachers, he would ensure that nothing unwholesome happened to the money. During such times, he remained composed and never gave off an impression that he had such a huge sum of money at home. It is a testament to his integrity that he never embezzled those teachers' salaries.

Even though he was not rich, my father was contended with what he. A striking incident that reinforced my father's honesty and commitment to his teaching career was when he had a financial problem. He had the teachers' salaries and could have used the money to resolve the matter and later replaced it. Instead, he harvested and sold cassava and yam tubers to raise the money he needed to resolve his financial issue.

I recall also one incident when the Schools' Board overpaid my father by thousands of naira. After paying all of the teachers and discovering that he was overpaid, my father returned the remaining balance to the Schools' Board. The director of the Schools' Board informed him that he had deliberately overpaid him to test his honesty. The director praised my father for passing the test and wondered at how great the world would be if people were like him.

Nothing Left Undone

Besides exemplifying his integrity to the public, my father also brought it home by teaching his children the importance of planning and self-dependence. One day, I urgently needed some money to register for the West African Senior School Certificate Examination, an examination I needed to enter a university in Nigeria. Being in the village, I did not realize that the registration for the examination had begun, and that I had only two days left to register for the examination before the deadline. At that time, my father was retired and did not have much money but was a secretary at a local association. Along with his new position as this association's secretary, he was responsible for safeguarding the association's monthly contributions. Since he had enough money from the contributions to cover my examination registration, I was counting on him giving me the money from the association's account to enable me meet up with the registration deadline. My plans were to harvest and sell cassava tubers to raise the money and replace it before the association needed it.

My father, however, refused to dip his hands into that account to assist me. Instead, he lectured me on the importance of planning, blaming me for not being careful enough to find out when the examination's registration began. He also told me that I could not plan my life on other people's resources. According to him, I could either raise the money to take care of my issues or forget about the issues until I was capable of raising the money. Adding that I must be responsible for my actions, he insisted that I raise the money by harvesting and selling cassava tubers within two days. As hard as it was, that was exactly what I did, and I have never forgotten that lecture. On many occasions in my adult life when the temptation to plan on other people's resources came up, I always overcame it. This is especially true if one is living in a place where a person can purchase almost everything on credit card and pay it back slowly.

I read about someone who bought items on her credit card worth three thousand dollars. When her credit card bill came, she did not have enough money to make the full payment. She then contacted the credit card company staff, who asked her to make a monthly minimum payment of twenty-five dollars and be charged a 25 percent interest. Since she did not have the money to cover the full payment, she accepted the offer and is paying back not only the three thousand dollars but also 25 percent interest on the bill. By the time she finishes the payment, she will have paid the credit card company an additional seven hundred and fifty dollars in interest charges. This is money that will be lost, which might have been used on other important things had she cut her coat according to her size.

If she continues to buy things on credit using her credit card, she will still be charged an additional 25 percent interest, with another minimum payment of twenty-five dollars per month. If she doesn't get a second job or cut down on her expenses, she will continue to be indebted for the rest of her life.

Personally, as tempting as the credit card offer is, I have never succumbed to purchasing things when I do not have the means to pay for them right away—thanks to my father. My husband and I are also instilling the same virtue in our children, hoping that they, too, can learn to spend within their means. By so doing, we can help pass down this legacy from generation to generation, just as my father encouraged me to.

As an authentic leader that he was, my father also taught me that diversity is strength, because it brings out the best in me. He always encouraged his children to respect one another's opinions and to value one another.

I learned from my father that through diversity, we are open to different perspectives on issues, which help to broaden our knowledge on the problems that we have. My father made it clear that in difficult situations, we must set aside our differences and embrace that which makes us unique—diversity. He also taught me that we must unify people and avoid speaking divisive words.

From touring different communities teaching, my father met people from different backgrounds, and he worked well with them. Through that and other actions, he set good examples for his children and those who looked up to him of why leadership matters and how diversity can bring love and unity to the world.

Having worked at U.S. embassies, I can clearly relate to my father's wisdom on diversity. In each country where I lived and worked, I met people from different backgrounds and perspectives. In my day-to-day interactions with them, I came to appreciate the importance of diversity in achieving a goal.

Perpetua Anaele

When people of various backgrounds and perspectives deliberate on an issue, they are likely to generate better ideas to solve a problem. A good leader celebrates diversity, as it helps to generate a plethora of opinions, bring unity, and empower and strengthen people in the same way my father envisioned the world could do.

CHAPTER 6

CHARACTER MATTERS

In 1994, when I was living with my oldest sister, Kate, in Port-Harcourt, my husband-to-be, having just flown in from the United States, briefly met me and proposed to marry me. The next day, one of my siblings visited me, informing me that my father needed to speak with me urgently. Ordinarily, I would have been worried about the topic of the discussion. In this case, however, I was not because I suspected that the discussion was related to the marriage proposal.

The next day, I arrived in the village, and everyone was pleased to see me. At night, my father invited me to his bedroom, and I knew right there that the discussion must be a big deal as it was to take place at such an ungodly hour and in such a private location. Nonetheless, I came in as he requested, and he asked me to sit down. As I sat down, he began to look at me squarely in the face, as if I had committed an offense.

Somewhat abashed, I asked, "What is it, Papa?"

"Well, my daughter, since you were born, I have never had this type of discussion with you; so, this is very important.

Perpetua Anaele

A man came here with his people yesterday, asking for your hand in marriage. Who is he, and how did you meet him?"

I told him how I met the man, and that it was okay to welcome him to the family.

"Is there a reason you are getting married now, my daughter? Did any member of the family offend you, or is someone pressuring you to get married to this man?"

"No, Papa. Nobody is pressuring me to do anything, and I have no problem with any member of the family. I just saw him; he proposed to me, and I accepted. I believe we can live peacefully together—the same way you've been living with Nmam."

"When he and his people came yesterday and told me the purpose of their visit, I told them that I needed to invite and hear from you, my daughter, before making any decision. Should I accept them? As you probably know, marriage is not the same as courtship. It is deeper than that. We are a Christian family. If there is any reason you wish not to marry this man, let me know right now."

I was grateful that my father took the time to speak to me, choosing to support my wishes in such a way both publicly and privately.

"I understand, Papa, and I thank you for first hearing from me before making a decision. Yes, please accept him and his family, and by the grace of God, we will live in peace."

Nothing Left Undone

"My daughter, since you have made up your mind to marry this man, allow me to tell you one or two things about marriage. In marriage, communication is very important; you must be open to your husband and ask him to do the same. Doing so will help to build trust between you two. You should love your husband, because, as a child of God, He wants you to love your fellow human being; do not attach any physical reason, such as wealth, to the love. Such a material thing will fade away with time, but if you truly love your husband, your love for him will be everlasting. No matter how he offends you, do not correct him in public; men have huge egos. If you challenge your husband publicly, you will damage his ego. Are you listening to me?"

"Yes, Papa."

"Good. Don't be a nag at home; no man likes a woman who complains all the time. Avoid being materialistic. By the grace of God, once you are married, you will begin having children for your husband; save for them and for a rainy day. Don't compare your husband to other men; everyone is different, and each circumstance is also different. Respect your husband. He chose you among other potential women; don't forget that. Include God in whatever you do; He will always see you through. Do you understand, my daughter?"

"Yes, Papa."

"Your mother and I have raised you well, and I know by the grace of God, you will succeed. This is it for now. Do you have any questions for me?"

Perpetua Anaele

"No, Papa. Thank you very much for everything. I am very grateful."

"You are welcome, my daughter, and good luck in life."

I then got up and left the room, very emotional. That night, I could not sleep. I reflected on the wonderful lessons of life my father had given me and wondered if my soon-to-be married life would be the same. Throughout the marriage preparation and on the day of the traditional marriage, he gave me his undivided attention, helping to ensure that the event was a success.

On the traditional marriage day, and in the heat of the ceremony, I introduced my husband-to-be to the entire community and brought him to my father for his blessing. My father then delivered an emotional speech, blessed us, took my hands, and handed me over to my husband. This was symbolic, as he was traditionally transferring my care and support to my husband. I was both happy and sad, and at night, I reflected on how my father had wonderfully raised his family, and I prayed to God to help me do the same for my family.

When I was growing up, my father set a standard on how a good Christian family should be, emphasizing on the need for his children to maintain good character traits. He never allowed us to disrespect one another or those outside of the family, and he never allowed us to display questionable behavior. For example, whenever I said something like, "Papa, I hate my English teacher, because he always gives me a lot of homework without regard to other classes that I am taking," my father would come back with, "There you go again, Perpetua. How many times have I told you to avoid using the word *hate*? Your teacher is helping to educate you, and as time goes on, you will be happy he did. Instead of complaining about the homework, why don't you create time to speak to him, making a case on why the assignment he is giving you is excessive and suggesting better ways to resolve the issue? Your teacher may not even be aware of the problem you are going through."

If I said, "My friend is in trouble with her mother, because she has refused to complete a household chore. As her friend, she has asked me to lie to her mother that she was unable to complete her chore because she was doing her homework with me." My father would say, "Instead of helping her by lying to her mother, why don't you help her by teaching her the importance of being truthful? Ask her to take responsibility for her actions by telling her mother the truth and apologizing for her behavior. Then, reward her for being honest by completing the chore with her."

Still, when I said, "My sister makes me mad by doing so and so," my father would remind me that nobody can make me mad unless I choose to be mad. I must admit that in those days, I felt that my father never let me off the hook, and I hated to seek advice from him sometimes. In hindsight, however, I now realize that he was laying down a foundation of great character for me and the rest of his children. He challenged us to be responsible for our actions, to be proactive, and to emulate integrity.

He made it clear then that character matters. "With a good character," he often said, "we can establish who we are in society and select the type of people we want to associate ourselves with. If we have a dishonorable character, chances are that people will not be drawn to us. We will likely be referred to as people who exhibit bad behavior. If we are of good character, on the other hand, people will be attracted to us and can defend us should we be wrongly accused of an offence. People will stand by us, arguing that the crime we are accused of is not in line with our character."

I recall a conversation I had with my father one Sunday evening. He was relaxing on his favorite chair near the kitchen while I peeled some oranges for him. "My daughter, there is nothing like a good name. With a good name, you can never go wrong. In our community, for example, people hear and talk about us. We also hear and talk about them. The question is what do they hear and say about us? Ensure that they talk about you positively. You must work hard to build a good name for yourself through the manner in which you carry yourself. When you live a life full of dignity and respect, people will associate themselves with you. If your character, on the other hand, is questionable, people will be uncomfortable of associating with you, as such an act could contaminate their character.

"It takes considerable time and energy for someone to build a good name, but it's very easy for the person to lose it. I have seen people who worked hard for years to make good names for themselves, only to lose them in seconds with a single bad act. So, as you build a respectable name for yourself,

Nothing Left Undone

work hard to maintain it. When you interact with people at church, school, work, or anywhere, ensure you conduct yourself with integrity and respect. Such behavior will live on in the hearts of people you associate with, creating a lasting impression of you."

My father was, indeed, a man of outstanding principle who exhibited great virtues, among them integrity, resolve, resourcefulness, courage, respect, consistency, and fortitude. He never deceived anyone or encouraged any of his children to do so. He maintained his stand even when doing so would cause him enormous discomfort.

One afternoon, he told me a story while washing his black Suzuki motorcycle. I was probably not yet born when he bought that motorcycle, but it still looked new then. He poured some Omo detergent into a bucket of water and dropped a washcloth and sponge into the bucket. Handing me a clean washcloth to hold for him and using his right hand, he agitated the water until it began to foam.

Turning to me, he said, "My daughter, never betray people who trust you with their resources."

As I looked on, he softly began to meticulously wash the motorcycle, as if he was bathing a newborn baby. He gently sponged different parts of the motorcycle, scrubbing the wheels carefully.

"You see," he continued, "as a headmaster, I pay teachers their salaries every month. These teachers depend on their incomes to sustain their families. A friend of mine visited me yesterday, asking me to loan him some money from the teachers' salaries. He told me he has an urgent family financial issue, and said he would repay me before the teachers pick up their salaries. My daughter, I cannot do that. What if I oblige him his request, and he refuses to comply with the terms of agreement? What will I say to the teachers happened to their salaries?"

"But Papa, he is your friend. I'm sure he will return the money before the teachers need it," I argued.

Signaling me to give him the clean washcloth, he said, "No, my daughter, I cannot compromise my integrity that way, friendship or no friendship."

As I handed him the washcloth, he began carefully drying the motorcycle with it while I continued to encourage him to help his friend. Placing the washcloth on the motorcycle and looking at me, he contended, "A true friend would never put his friend in trouble. I have asked my friend to take half of my salary and find the rest of the money he needs elsewhere, but he has adamantly refused. He wants me to give him the full amount, which I do not have. I am very upset that he made such an outrageous request in the first place, and there is no way I can maintain my relationship with him at the expense of the teachers' salaries."

Bottom line, my father never complied with his friend's request.

Years ago, he also told me a story of a man who—in his quest to assume a higher position with the government—pleaded with him to falsify a document that would enable him to achieve his selfish desire. As I understood it, my father was in a position to assist this man if he had wanted to. However, my father told him that he would not compromise his character by lying. He reminded the man that the position in question was rotated among qualified people every two years, and that it was not his turn to assume the position that year. He encouraged the man to wait until his turn before seeking the position and his help.

The man, however, vehemently refused to listen to my father; instead, he promised to enrich my father if his wish was granted. My father declined his offer, letting the man know that he preferred to die a poor man rather than become rich in a dishonest way. Although his refusal cost him his long-term relationship with his friend, my father felt that maintaining his integrity was far more important than the relationship.

It is through my father's virtue of integrity that the people in his community normally came to him when they needed to clarify an issue. They would often say, "Let's go to Sir Nwosu. He will be the one to clarify this issue. If he says the answer is A, that's exactly what it is."

In addition, during farming seasons in the village, I had seen many families quarreling and fighting over a piece of land. Some argued that the land belonged to their great-grandparents and now belong to them. Some would fight over a small portion or a demarcation of the land, ending up physically injuring their family members or arresting them. Others would consult native doctors, asking their family members to swear an oath for them. In such volatile situations, people would come to my father to help them locate the actual boundary of the land or, at least, help them to achieve a peaceful resolution. He never wavered in providing amicable solutions to such issues.

My father displayed great resolve in his lifetime. While growing up, he faced some challenges along the way, but he never gave up. For example, his mother died when he was very young; his four siblings also died, making him the only surviving family member then.

When he got married and started raising a family, he lost his six-year-old son, Vanacious. This was a tremendous loss given that Vanacious was his first son and died just after the family had returned from the civil war in 1970.

Instead of giving up on life, my father turned these setbacks into triumphs, accepting his fate and working hard to change the trajectory of his life. He used these impediments to become an agent for change, mentoring people who were going through similar issues in life. My father became an active member of the Roman Catholic Church, dedicating part of his time to serving Catholic missionaries. He interpreted and translated for them and served the church during Mass. The priests trusted him enough to assign him various tasks, including safeguarding the church offerings; in line with his trait of integrity, he never tampered with the church offerings.

My Father-Second in the Front Row from Right-
with Catholic Priests and Teachers, 1957

As human beings, we all make mistakes, but what separated my father from most people was that he recognized his mistakes and did something about them. I recall one day when he paid a teacher short by mistake. Using his payment list, he had an idea which teacher he had done so to. He quickly contacted the individual and assisted him in recounting the money. When he did, he confirmed the mistake, resolved the issue, and apologized to the teacher. The teacher was grateful. This is remarkable; many people in my father's position would have kept the remaining money and used it to take care of some personal needs.

Mr. Nwosu was a very resourceful man. Although he was not rich, he was not covetous of other people's belongings; he never envied people or wished to possess their possessions. Instead of not getting enough resources to sustain his family, he hustled daily to make a living. When the government delayed in paying teachers their salaries, my father relied on farming to keep the family going. If the farming was not enough, he sold kerosene and fuel to augment the farming income. At times, he harvested some plantain from his plantation and some coconut, selling them at the local market. My father never depended on other people's resources to survive. He knew God had given him enough resources to take care of his family, and he took advantage of such resources. In return, God blessed him abundantly.

Mr. Nwosu's magnanimity was unquestionable. He showed kindness to people of all ages. Young people would come to him for advice, and he would mentor them, as if they were his children. He encouraged them to go to school and become meaningful members of society. At times, when parents asked him to counsel their children with whom they were having problems, my father gladly did so, eventually becoming friends to those very children. People in his community sought his guidance from time to time, and he never disappointed them.

After my father passed away in 2017, I met a woman who told me a story of an encounter she'd had with my father. She explained that even though she was married, her husband cared neither for her nor for her children. She added that in an effort to unjustly punish her, her husband married other women and refused to assign her a piece of land on which she could farm and feed her children. One day, she neither had food to eat nor money to buy food at the market. Having heard from her friends of how my father had assisted them one way or another, she decided to try her luck. On arriving at my father's house, she said she began to cry, informing him of her dire situation. My father immediately

Nothing Left Undone

told her to stop crying and that as long as he was alive, she and her children would not go to bed hungry. He then gave her some money to buy some food for the night and directed her to go to his farm the next day to harvest some cassava tubers. She did, and after selling the cassava tubers, she was able to get enough money to take care of her family.

My father's kindness also extended to him encouraging us, his children, to donate our lightly used clothes to the less privileged in the community. In those days, during New Year's Eve, we ushered in a New Year by burning our old clothes and throwing away food from the year that had just ended. We did that from year to year as a way to let go of bad things from the old year and usher in good things for the New Year.

One year, however, my father suggested that instead of us burning our lightly used clothes, why don't we donate them to the less privileged? We felt it was a good idea, and since then, we not only began donating the clothes to those who needed them, but we also started providing food to the needy. What joy I felt one day when I delivered some food and clothes to a poor widow! She tightly hugged me and asked me to thank my father on her behalf.

As adults, my husband and I have continued to uphold this legacy of charity, donating money and food to the less privileged and at times, visiting orphanages and hospitals with our children.

It took guts for my father to undertake some of the actions he took in his lifetime. For example, he decided to pursue

Perpetua Anaele

his career as a teacher during a period when people did not consider such an option. He was courageous enough to map out a plan for achieving his goal, and he also followed it through. He interpreted for white missionaries and traveled far and near to teach and mold the characters of young people. In situations when he defended the truth, letting people know what they were doing was wrong, it took courage for him to do so.

In his letter to the Colossians, Saint Paul urged them to "rid [themselves] of all such things as these: anger, rage, malice, slander, and filthy language from [their] lips" (Colossians 3:8). He also asked them to avoid lying and to forgive one another, encouraging them to clothe themselves with "compassion, kindness, humility, gentleness, and patience" (v. 12).

My father embodied that type of life when he was alive. He was very humble and calm in dealing with people. I used to wonder why in the heat of an argument, my father remained so tranquil. He would not say a word, but later when everyone was at ease, he would then express his opinion. Although my father's idea of remaining peaceful in the heat of an argument was hard medicine for me to swallow, as an adult, I have seen the wisdom in his behavior. In those days, when he finally said something, people were calm enough to listen to and reason with him.

I read that one of America's presidents, President Harry S. Truman, had a rule during his presidency: for twenty-four hours, he kept on his desk any letter he wrote out of anger. After twenty-four hours, if he was still upset, he would mail the letter, but if he cooled off, he never mailed the letter. By the time he finished his presidency, his un-mailed letters filled a large desk drawer. It is difficult for us to do so anymore, given today's immediate communication. If we can wait for an ordinary twenty-four hours before reacting, however, we can avoid causing ourselves an embarrassment.

All too often, some people jump to a conclusion without getting the facts of the matter. They wrongly accuse others, lashing out in anger, only to realize that the accused person is innocent.

During my undergraduate program, a friend of mine accused her roommate of stealing her money. Despite her roommate's plea of innocence, my friend publicized the issue to her other friends, gossiping and damaging her roommate's reputation. Out of anger, her roommate moved out of the room, and a week later, my friend found her money in one of her handbags. Apparently, she had left the money there some weeks back without realizing it. Consequently, she was so embarrassed at her behavior that she did not let the roommate know she had found the money. Had she believed her roommate and calmed down enough to carefully look for the money, she would have found it, and the damage that followed would have been prevented.

Having come across the biblical quotations below, I became convinced that my father's stance of composure in the heat of an argument is the right thing to do:

- "A quick-tempered person does foolish things, and the one who devises evil schemes is hated" (Proverbs 14:17).

- "He who answers a matter before he hears it, that is folly and shame to him" (Proverbs 18:13).
- "Those who guard their lips preserve their lives, but those who speak rashly will come to ruin" (Proverbs 13:3).
- "The tongue has the power of life and death, and those who love it will eat its fruit" (Proverbs 18:21).
- "My dear brothers and sisters, take note of this: Everyone should be quick to listen, slow to speak, and slow to become angry" (James 1:19).

Following the human tendency, some people are often inclined to react in anger, making a mess of an already fragile situation. My father, however, taught me and other members of the family not to react in anger, as we could worsen the problem and later be in a position to apologize. He advised us to speak words of encouragement to others and not words that demoralize them.

"Watch your tongue," he often advised. "Speak only when necessary, and think before you speak. The tongue is a dangerous weapon; it can build or destroy. Do not speak hateful words or give violent speeches. Avoid the use of curse words. Do not insult people by what you say. Be careful of how you use your words, because that can reflect who you are. Spoken words can come to pass, so carefully choose what to say, focusing on positive words at all times. If you guard what you say, the world will be a better place for all."

My father skillfully mastered the ability of living in harmony with people, and that helped him live a fruitful life. Throughout his life, I cannot remember any day he

Nothing Left Undone

pressed charges on anyone or had a court case with another. My father never took sides or carried out any action that had the effect of fanning the flame of hate.

He also refused to jump to conclusions without knowing the facts of an issue. He avoided having preconceived thoughts about people without first hearing the facts and knowing exactly where they were coming from. My father knew that doing otherwise could lead to serious misconceptions.

This legacy was handy to me some years ago. My husband and I had just bought our first house. In America, it is considered a big deal for one to own a house, so we were, undeniably, excited. After buying the house, we purchased thousands of dollars' worth of household furniture and appliances to decorate the house. To show gratitude for the amount of money we had spent at the store, the store manager decided to provide us free delivery service for our purchased items.

On the day of the furniture delivery, I mistakenly left my jewelry box on the bedroom dresser. The jewelry box was very important, because it contained beautiful jewelry. As the movers came, I was so occupied with the moving that I did not remember to remove the jewelry box from the dresser. Two days later, when I was getting ready to go to church, I began looking for the jewelry box. I searched everywhere in the house but could not find it. The next day, I continued to search for it but to no avail.

I then concluded that one of the movers had taken the jewelry box. Being very upset, I decided to contact the store

Perpetua Anaele

manager to complain. However, I asked myself, "What would my father do in this situation?" I then reasoned that he would be patient to search for the missing jewelry box more carefully, and if he could not find it, he would gently ask the movers if they had seen it in the house; he would never wrongly accuse anyone.

After carefully deliberating on this, I decided to look for the jewelry box again. Funny enough, I found it under my bed. Apparently, the movers had mistakenly dropped it under the bed while they were moving our things in. Considering that one could be sued for wrongly accusing another, I thanked my God for giving me such a superb father. Since that day, I avoid jumping to conclusions without first knowing the facts of a matter.

When I was growing up, my father also always cautioned me and the rest of his children to avoid appearing boastful. "In an effort to innocently showcase your achievements, you could appear proud, and someone could misinterpret it, becoming envious, and then seeking to make your lives miserable," he often warned.

Considering the story of Joseph in Genesis of the Holy Bible, I cannot agree more. Joseph was the eleventh son of Jacob or Israel and his mother, Rachel, was his father's favorite wife. His ten brothers were half-brothers from three stepmothers. His mother was barren for years, but in his father's old age, she bore Joseph as her first son. Then, after the birth of her second child, Benjamin, she died. Because Joseph was born in his father's old age to a woman he loved so dearly, his father loved him passionately. His father made him a coat of many colors and never hid his love for him from his other children.

Realizing that their father loved Joseph more than he loved them, his ten half-brothers hated him and did not speak kindly to him (Genesis, 37:3–4). This was the beginning of Joseph's problem. Then, Joseph had a dream and told his brothers about it: "We were binding sheaves of grain out in the field when suddenly my sheaf rose and stood upright, while your sheaves gathered around mine and bowed down to it" (v. 7).

After he told his brothers the dream, they were even more furious. "'Do you intend to reign over us? Will you actually rule us?' And they hated him all the more because of his dream and what he had said" (v. 8).

Still, Joseph had another dream and told it to his brothers, saying, "I had another dream, and this time the sun and moon and eleven stars were bowing down to me" (v. 9).

He told the dream to his father also, who rebuked him, asking if he, his mother, and brothers would worship him (v. 10). Since the significance of Joseph's dream was that he was going to be someone greater than his parents and his brothers, his brothers naturally became envious of him.

One day, his brothers went to feed their father's flock in the fields, and their father sent Joseph to check on them. As he went, his brothers sighted him from afar and began plotting to kill him. One of his half-brothers, Reuben, heard the conspiracy and discouraged them from killing him. He

Perpetua Anaele

suggested that since he was their brother, instead of killing him, they should put him in a pit. They agreed to do so, but Reuben was secretly planning to save him from the pit once all the half-brothers were gone.

When Joseph innocently came to his brothers, they stripped him of his colorful coat and threw him inside an empty hole. They left him there and began to eat their bread. Then, they saw some Midianite traders who were going to Egypt to sell their goods. One of his brothers, Judah, had a different thought. He said to his brothers, "What will we gain if we kill our brother and cover up his blood? Come, let's sell him to the Ishmaelites and not lay our hands on him; after all, he is our brother, our own flesh and blood" (vs. 26–27). They brought Joseph out from the pit and sold him to the traders for twenty pieces of silver, and the traders took him to Egypt.

Reuben, being unaware of what had transpired, returned to the pit to rescue Joseph, but he was no longer there. Reuben became very upset and returned to his brothers, informing them that he could not find Joseph in the pit. The brothers then killed a goat and rubbed the blood on Joseph's coat and took it home to Israel, their father, asking him whether it was Joseph's coat. He said it was and concluded that a wild animal had killed Joseph. Israel was very upset, tearing his clothes and putting sackcloth upon his loins. For days, he cried and mourned for the death of Joseph. His children tried to console him, but he refused to be consoled.

Meanwhile, the Midianites, who had bought Joseph from his brothers, sold him in Egypt to Potiphar, a man who worked for Pharaoh, the king of Egypt. Potiphar was the officer of Pharaoh's guard; thus, Joseph became a slave in Egypt—and the story continued.

This story is, indeed, an eye-opener to the challenges we face in this world. The pit is a metaphor for our worldly issue. It can take the form of divorce, death, injury, debt, job loss, and another challenge. In most cases, it happens without any warning. Joseph never expected such a disaster to befall him that day, but it did. When an unforeseen circumstance occurs, it changes our lives immediately. Joseph's life instantly turned upside down as soon as he was thrown into that pit. While in the pit, he was probably shocked and could not believe what he was going through. He must have felt inconceivable pain, anger, and betrayal. Joseph, undoubtedly, could not believe what his brothers were doing to him. He possibly realized that he was in a pit and knew why he was there.

For us, while in the pit, we need to recognize where we are and reflect on how we got there to begin with. Our recognition of where we are and how we got there are important steps toward our getting out of the pit. Also, in our sober reflection, we need to remember that sometimes, God allows us to fall into a pit to teach us something. At times, however, we are in a pit due to our character or action. For example, due to our lack of proper investment, we can end up in a pit of indebtedness. It could also be that we never took our employment seriously, and we end up in a pit of unemployment. Whatever reason it might be, in most cases, the warning signs are usually there, but we somehow ignore them until it is too late.

In the case of Joseph, for example, he was arrogant and as a result, he was not sensitive to his brothers' feelings before telling them the dreams he had. What his brothers did was wrong, but Joseph shared some part of the blame too. He could have humbled himself by being quiet without appearing boastful, but because he encouraged his brothers to believe that he felt superior to them, they conspired to make his life miserable. My father always preached that his children be humble. The impact of Joseph's lack of humility is a typical example of why we should be humble.

Joseph's story is a constant reminder of the need for us to have a good character and to be sensitive to people's feelings. In dealing with people, we should be observant and know when not to cross the line. The first time Joseph had a dream and explained it to his brothers, he should have noticed their reactions and then avoided telling them the second dream. Because he was not careful enough to notice that his brothers were envious of him, he went ahead and told them both dreams, infuriating them in the process and soon finding himself in a pit.

My father taught me that as we humans model good character, we can avoid falling into a pit. If we still do, by realizing our mistakes and learning from them, we can get out of whatever pit we find ourselves in as soon as possible.

CHAPTER 7

FORGIVENESS IS FREEDOM

It was a chilly Monday afternoon. I had just returned from primary school, very tired and hungry. As I arrived at my father's compound, I noticed an unusual number of people gathered. Some were crying, and others were whispering to each other, but the moment they saw me enter the compound, they all grew quiet.

"What's going on here?" I said.

They looked at each other and then looked away, as if they did not understand my question. Quickly, I dropped my schoolbag on the floor and ran toward my father's living room. As I was heading there, I noticed that the room was crowded with many people who were crying, but I could not figure out what was going on.

Anxious about what the issue was, I asked, "Can someone please tell me what's going on? Did someone die? Where is Papam? Nma, where are you?"

Still, no response. Suddenly, a woman took my hands and said, "It's well, my daughter. He will be all right."

"What do you mean he will be all right? Who is 'he,' and what happened to him?"

"Your father."

"Yes, please go on. What happened to him?"

"He was involved in a serious motorcycle accident this afternoon on his way back from the farm, and his right leg is, unfortunately, broken. He is bleeding a lot, and people are trying to help control the amount of blood he is losing."

Pushing the woman aside, I made my way to where my father was, screaming, "Papa, where are you?" Immediately, I saw my father in a pool of blood, crying for help; he was obviously in pain. I began to cry, and people pulled me aside. As I was crying, I saw the rest of my family members weeping and consoling our father. I also saw some people tying strips of cloth on my father's affected leg. Those helping my father then put him on a motorcycle and took him to a nearby clinic.

While my father was still receiving some treatment at the clinic, some people were gathering in there to see him, and others were coming to our compound to offer us their condolences.

A week later, my father was recovering well. Then, there was an issue of arresting the man from Umuoye, a neighboring community, who had hit my father and ran away. When my father was at the clinic, the family members of the man who had injured him came and pleaded on behalf of their son. As my father returned from the clinic, they came again, apologizing. "Please forgive and forget," they said. "We could not bring him with us, because he was afraid you would arrest him or have your family beat him up."

Surprisingly, my father told them that what had taken place was an accident, which could happen to anyone. He also told them that he had already forgiven the young man. The man's relatives were happy. They asked to reimburse my father's treatment bill, but he refused.

A few days later, the man who had injured my father came, thanking my father for his kindness. Apparently, he was drunk the day of the accident and was not in his right mind. My father advised him to quit drinking, as the accident could have been fatal. He thanked my father for his advice, promising to take it seriously and later left.

Once he departed, some of my father's friends, who saw what had happened, blamed him for not taking the matter up, or for at least, not allowing the man to cover his treatment bill. My father, however, emphasized that what had happened to him was an accident, which could happen to anyone.

One important virtue I learned from my father was the need to exercise restraint, forgiving anyone who wrongs me. Throughout my upbringing, my father inculcated this virtue in his children, emphasizing that as humans, we are imperfect and, therefore, err. He did this through his biblical advice and numerous life experiences. Setting himself as an example, he quickly made up with people who offended him. On several occasions, he said, "Forgiveness is freedom, and we cannot be free unless we forgive those who have wronged us."

While growing up, I noticed that some people would miscalculate my father's meekness for weakness and try to push the envelope. My father, on the other hand, would often show very skillful leadership, applying diplomacy backed by wisdom and avoiding succumbing to their demands. He maintained peace with them, forgiving them even if they did not deserve it or ask to be forgiven.

In February 2015, Bro. Polly was kidnapped. He suffered greatly at the hands of his kidnappers. Our family also went through enormous psychological and emotional turmoil.

The kidnappers threatened daily to take Bro. Polly's life if we did not provide them five million naira, which was equivalent to about fourteen thousand U.S. dollars. They would speak only with one of our sisters, Sister Ange, threatening, "Provide us the money today, or you will find your brother's dead body on the road." At times, they would hand the phone to Bro. Polly and quickly snatch it back from him the moment Sister Ange heard him cry for help. It was an emotional torture—one I do not wish on anyone.

Since my family could not come up with their demand, Sister Ange pleaded with them to reduce the amount to what we could afford. They did, but when our family provided them the money, they still refused to release Bro. Polly as promised.

Nothing Left Undone

"Do you think we are stupid?" their spokesman asked. "You hate your brother so much that you cannot come up with an ordinary five million naira. If you do not provide that money by tomorrow, you will find Pollycap's body parts scattered along the road," he threatened.

It was a confusing situation. While the police officers, who were tasked with locating our brother, discouraged us from paying the ransom, other people in Obite community suggested that we provide the kidnappers the money to save our brother's life. Our family rallied around and raised the money. However, the day the money was to be delivered to the criminals—which was the same day they had intended to kill our brother—miraculously, the police found them sharing the money the family had already given them. The police then apprehended about eight of them while others escaped. The police also released our brother.

About two weeks after being released, Bro. Polly requested that the kidnappers be set free, citing that vengeance belongs to the Lord. I was flabbergasted. "How could you ask the police to release those criminals?" I asked. "Since they did not get the five million naira they demanded, don't you know they may return for another family member?" But Bro. Polly's decision was final, and the kidnappers were all released.

A few months later, on September 20, 2015, my worst fear came true, crushing down on me as another group of kidnappers, or possibly the same group that had kidnapped our brother, came and abducted our mother. This was more profound, given that our mother was taking care of our aged father in the village when the incident happened. The kidnappers mercilessly pushed our father down on his bed, despite his crying and pleading to them to leave his wife alone. They wickedly blindfolded our mother, took her to an unknown place, and fired gunshots on their way out.

A day after the kidnapping, they contacted us, requesting five million naira from the family. In the heat of the turmoil, I called my father on the phone from the United States to encourage him to hang in there. Extraordinarily, he was simply singing his favorite church song:

In the hollow of His hand,
In the hollow of His hand,
I am safe while God himself doth hold me,
In the hollow of His hand.

After listening to him sing, I was motivated to be hopeful and strong. Following a series of negotiations, our family provided the kidnappers with what we could afford, and a week later, they released our mother unharmed. Thankfully, the police apprehended them as well, and in line with our forgiveness virtue, we forgave the kidnappers. However, the authorities in Nigeria refused to release them, stating that they were a nuisance to the public.

I must admit that forgiving can be very difficult. While growing up, I never paid much attention to my father's preaching on forgiveness, as I could not possibly understand why I would forgive someone who had knowingly wronged me, especially if the person neither repented from the wrongdoing nor asked for my forgiveness. In my adult years, however, I began to research my father's biblical basis for emphasizing that we forgive those who have wronged us; I began to understand, based on the information below, that forgiveness is, indeed, freedom, and to be free, we must forgive our offenders.

We should forgive, because God asks us to. God knows how difficult it is for us to forgive others, but He still wants us to do so. In Matthew 18:21–22, Peter asks Jesus, "Lord, how many times shall I forgive my brother or sister who sins against me? Up to seven times?"

Jesus answers, "I tell you, not seven times, but seventy-seven times."

In other words, Jesus is asking us to forgive others who have wronged us no matter what. He knows that as human beings, we are likely to have some disagreements, but He insists that we forgive those who have done us wrong. Jesus wants us to forgive habitually.

When someone offends us, we have the tendency to avenge, but 1 Peter 3:9 says, "Do not repay evil with evil or insult with insult. On the contrary, repay evil with blessing, because to this you were called so that you may inherit a blessing."

In his letter to the Ephesians, Paul made it clear that they need to "[b]e kind and compassionate to one another, forgiving each other, just as in Christ God forgave [them]" (Ephesians 4:32).

We should forgive, because forgiveness is reciprocal. As humans, we tend to surrender to our feeling toward anger, hatred, and revenge for injustices perpetrated against us; we forget that we also make mistakes. If we cannot forgive someone who offended us, why should we ask to be forgiven when we offend someone else?

We should forgive, because we deserve to be at peace. Forgiveness sets us free from having bitter thoughts about anyone who has offended us. The reason is that when someone offends us, we often think about how the person has wronged us, and we tend to hold onto ill feelings and hatred. If the person repents and seeks our forgiveness but we refuse to forgive, we are hurting ourselves even more.

We should forgive those who wronged us to avoid unintentionally harming ourselves. Hatred and anger are detrimental to our health. When we bear grudges against those who have offended us, we, accidentally, bring harm to ourselves. If we do so, it becomes a double jeopardy, because we are not only angry with the person who offended us, but we are also indirectly releasing toxins into our bodies by refusing to forgive. When we are sad, our bodies, including our brains, react that way, leading to illnesses, such as high blood pressure and depression. On the other hand, when we are happy, our bodies also react that way, releasing dopamine, a pleasure hormone, which makes us glow. This is why experts recommend that we do things that make us happy at all times. Being unforgiving is certainly not one of them.

Besides, if someone consciously offends us, he or she wants us to be in a state of bitterness. If we realize this and do the opposite, the one who offended us will be disappointed, and his or her plan to make us unhappy will have been defeated. This is also the same tactic the devil uses to attack us. It is up to us to realize this and do the opposite of what the devil intends.

We should forgive, because if we choose not to, we are offending God. God is love and can forgive anyone who sincerely repents. When someone offends us and seeks our forgiveness but we refuse to forgive, the person can seek God's forgiveness. If God forgives him or her, the individual is forgiven indeed. No matter how many times we ask God to avenge for us, He will not listen. In fact, we will be offending God for not forgiving the person who has wronged us.

We should forgive, because when we make our supplications to God without forgiving someone who has wronged us, God will not answer such prayers. In Matthew 6:14–15, the Bible makes it clear that "[f]or if you forgive other people when they sin against you, your heavenly Father will also forgive you. But if you do not forgive others their sins, your Father will not forgive your sins."

We should forgive, because vengeance is the Lord's. It does not matter if the person who offended us repents or not, we still need to forgive. Since vengeance belongs to God, it is up to Him to either forgive that person or not; we must not take matters into our hands by not forgiving. Instead, we should forgive and pray to God to do the same to our offenders.

Perpetua Anaele

In Luke 23:34, Jesus teaches us the act of forgiveness during his crucifixion. Despite the agony He was going through at the hands of those He had not wronged, He still prayed for them, "Father, forgive them; for they do not know what they are doing."

We should forgive because when we do, we are really not changing what the person did to us. Rather, we are paving the way for future relationships with our offenders. What actually changes when we forgive is that we no longer hate the person for what he or she has done, and we release all negative thoughts about the individual.

We should forgive if we are courageous. I must admit that it takes an immense amount of effort for us to actually forgive those who have hurt us. However, some people feel that those who forgive are cowards; that they are not strong enough to keep malice. On the contrary, forgiveness takes a lot of courage to carry out, and only courageous people are capable of forgiving.

We should forgive, because there is an enormous joy that comes with it. In my experience, I have often felt a great sense of relief when I forgave someone who had wronged me.

Years ago, at work, my coworker accused me of stealing a very important piece of equipment we were working with. The equipment was so important that if lost, it would cost our office a lot of money. On hearing this, I went to my supervisor and informed her that I did not steal that equipment, that in fact I was brought up not to steal, and that there was no way I could begin stealing in my adult

Nothing Left Undone

years. She refused to listen to me. Instead, she threatened that if I did not produce that equipment within a week, I would see the other side of her.

At home, I narrated the incident to my family, and we all prayed about it. Before the end of the week, the coworker who had accused me of stealing the equipment, came to me apologizing. When I asked her why she was sorry, she said she had found the missing equipment; that in fact, she had used it last and never remembered to put it back where it was supposed to be. Minutes after she apologized, my supervisor called me to her office and also tendered her apology.

I was speechless throughout the incident. I came home that day furious, wanting to bring the matter up to our higher authorities. But later, I asked myself what my father would have done under the same conditions. I clearly knew that the answer would be to forgive and move on, so that was exactly what I did. After forgiving my coworker and my supervisor, I felt an incredible sense of relief and an overwhelming peace. While at work, some friends continued to pressure me to take the matter to my higher ups, but I refused.

Unquestionably, issues arise in families, but such issues should not be allowed to escalate to irreparable damage. God created families and appreciates it if their members live in harmony and worship Him. The devil recognizes the importance of families to God. This is why he attacks families and by so doing, he tries to bring dishonor to God.

While I was growing up, my father often reminded us, his children, of the importance of living peacefully with and forgiving each other. His lesson on forgiveness mirrors the excerpt below from Pope Francis, and it is my hope that everyone can implement this legacy of forgiveness.

"There is no perfect family.
We do not have perfect parents.
We are not perfect.
We do not marry a perfect person, or we do not have perfect children.
We have complaints from each other.
We are constantly disappointed.
There is no healthy marriage or healthy family without the exercise of forgiveness.
Forgiveness is vital to our emotional health and spiritual survival. Without forgiveness, the family becomes an arena of conflict and a fortress of evil.
Without forgiveness, the family becomes sick.
Forgiveness is the asepsis of the soul, the purification of the spirit, and the liberation of the heart.
He who does not forgive does not have peace in his soul or communion with God.
Evil is a poison that intoxicates and kills.
Keeping heartache in your heart is a self-destructive gesture. It's autophagy.
Those who do not forgive are physically, emotionally and spiritually ill. For this reason, the family must be a place of life and not a place of death; a place of paradise and not a place of hell; a healing territory and not a disease; an internship of forgiveness and not guilt.

Forgiveness brings joy where sorrow has brought sadness; of the healing where sorrow has caused the disease" (Pope Francis, 2017 Message on Family).

God allows certain things to happen to us, so we can learn and grow from them. In such situations, He always wants us to forgive our offenders. The story of Joseph in Genesis is an example of this. Joseph became a slave in Egypt in the house of Potiphar. This was a great betrayal by his brothers, and they never had any remorse for their actions even after selling him. Instead, they lied to their aged father about Joseph's whereabouts. They did not care how their brother was faring in a foreign land. They pretended that everything was normal and never bothered to look for their brother. This was totally wicked.

While Joseph was in Egypt, God was with him, and he became prosperous in his master's house. The master noticed that God was with Joseph in that whatever he did, he prospered. Joseph served his master very well, respecting him; in turn, his master favored him, promoting him to be the overseer of his household and of everything he had. God blessed Potiphar even more because of the presence of Joseph in his house.

Even though Joseph came out of the first pit, he soon found himself in another pit. Potiphar's wife tempted him, asking him to sleep with her. Joseph refused, citing that it was sinful in the sight of God. He also stated that his master had trusted him enough to make him the overseer of his household, and there was no way he could betray him. The woman never gave up. She continued to pressure Joseph day by day to sleep with her, but he resisted.

One day, as Joseph was alone in one of the rooms, working for his master, the master's wife came in, held on to his garment, and insisted that he sleep with her. Joseph refused and ran out of the room, leaving his garment behind. Then, the woman came up with a perfect plan: "When she saw that he had left his cloak in her hand and had run out of the house, she called her household servants. 'Look,' she said to them, 'this Hebrew has been brought to us to make sport of us! He came in there to sleep with me, but I screamed. When he heard me scream for help, he left this cloak beside me and ran out of the house'" (Genesis 39:13–16).

When her husband came back, she lied to him that Joseph had tried to sleep with her. The husband was upset, feeling betrayed that Joseph could not respect him enough to stay away from his wife. Without investigating what actually happened, however, he put Joseph in prison, the same place where Pharaoh's prisoners were kept.

God continued to bless Joseph while he was in prison. Joseph found favor with the captain of the prisoners, who made him overseer of the other prisoners. He carried out his duties scrupulously, looking after the welfare of his fellow prisoners.

One day, Pharaoh's chief butler and chief baker, after offending Pharaoh, their master, were imprisoned in the same prison where Joseph was. Because it was Joseph's duty to oversee all prisoners, the captain of the guards

Nothing Left Undone

assigned the two prisoners to him as well. One night, the new prisoners each had a dream, and in the morning, they were upset, because nobody could interpret their dreams for them. Joseph, while discharging his duty in the morning, noticed that they were sad, and he inquired from them why they were distraught. The prisoners explained to him that they each had a dream, but nobody could interpret it for them. Joseph then informed them that only God could interpret their dreams.

When Joseph later asked the chief butler to tell him the dream, the chief butler said, "In my dream I saw a vine in front of me, and on the vine were three branches. As soon as it budded, it blossomed, and its clusters ripened into grapes. Pharaoh's cup was in my hand, and I took the grapes, squeezed them into Pharaoh's cup and put the cup in his hands" (Genesis 40:9–11). Joseph interpreted the dream, informing the chief butler that in three days, Pharaoh would release him from the prison and restore his position as a chief butler. He also asked the chief butler to remember to tell Pharaoh about him (Joseph) once he was out of the prison. The chief butler promised to do so. The chief baker then narrated his dream to Joseph, and Joseph interpreted it to mean that in three days, Pharaoh would kill him.

Later, Joseph's interpretation of the dreams came to pass, but the chief butler forgot to mention him to Pharaoh as he had promised. He abandoned Joseph in prison for two years. While in the prison, Joseph persevered. He never lost hope that one day God would save him. He never complained about how deplorable his life had been. Instead,

Perpetua Anaele

he continued to discharge his duties to other inmates. By so doing, he engaged himself during his trial.

The lesson I learned from my father from this part of Joseph's story is that even if my condition is appalling, I should find some activities in which to engage myself. For example, I can choose to serve others who are going through the same problems that I am experiencing. When my father lost his first son and was going through various life challenges, he never gave up. Instead, he began helping those who were undergoing challenges, mentoring them to be teachers and contributors of nation-building. Likewise, Joseph, despite everything that had happened to him, was serving his fellow prisoners.

Then, one day, Pharaoh had a dream and nobody could interpret it for him. At last, the chief butler remembered Joseph and told Pharaoh about him. Joseph was brought from the prison to Pharaoh, and with the help of God, he interpreted the dream to Pharaoh, stating that for seven years, there would be a surplus of food in Egypt followed by seven years of famine. Before interpreting the dream, he told Pharaoh that it is God who interprets dreams. He brought God to the attention of Pharaoh, letting him know how wonderful He is.

Besides his interpretation, Joseph also advised Pharaoh about what to do to ensure that Egypt took advantage of God's warning in the dream. Pharaoh said to Joseph, "Since God has made all this known to you, there is no one so discerning and wise as you. You shall be in charge of my palace, and all my people are to submit to your orders. Only with respect to the throne will I be greater than you" (Genesis 41:39–40). Pharaoh took a ring from his hand and put it on Joseph's hand. Then, he ordered that Joseph be given fine robes to wear and gold to wear around his neck. Pharaoh gave him a chariot to ride in as his second-in-command, and people bowed in worship of Joseph, calling him a ruler over Egypt. Pharaoh even changed Joseph's name and gave him a woman to marry.

The story of Joseph continued to where he safeguarded food in Egypt, and Pharaoh's dream came to pass. Later, there was famine across the world, to the point that Joseph's brothers came to Egypt in search of food. On arriving there, they did not recognize their brother, Joseph, but he recognized them. Later, in the story, his brothers bowed down to worship him without realizing that he was Joseph, confirming the dreams he'd had years before (Genesis 43:26).

We also read from Genesis 45 that Joseph later revealed himself to his brothers, forgave them, and asked the entire family to live with him in Egypt. While in Egypt, he took good care of them, and with approval from Pharaoh, he gave them a fertile part of the country, Goshen, in which to live and take care of their flock. Later, their father, Israel, passed away, and Joseph's brothers were still afraid that with their father's passing, Joseph would retaliate for what they did to him. They sent a message to him, letting him know that their father had asked him to forgive them before he passed.

Joseph reassured his brothers that he had forgiven them, saying, "You intended to harm me, but God intended it for good to accomplish what is now being done, the saving of many lives. So then, don't be afraid. I will provide for you and your children." "And he reassured them and spoke kindly to them" (Genesis, 50:20–21).

This is an amazing story of forgiveness. Joseph forgave all. He reconciled with his family and even took care of them in a foreign land.

One important lesson we learned from the story of Joseph is that when things begin to work well for us, we need to reconcile with those who mistreated us. It is not time for revenge but time for making peace with the people who wronged us. Joseph forgave his brothers and restored his relationship with them. In Genesis 45:2–7, Joseph introduced himself to his brothers, weeping and asking them not to be angry with themselves for what they had done. He reassured them that what they had done was part of God's plan for him to preserve a posterity on earth and to save their lives. He wept for the love he had for them and for the joy of reconciliation.

The story of Joseph also teaches us that when we are no longer in the pit, we must not forget what we learned there. God teaches us many lessons while we struggle. It could be to love, to be patient, to trust Him, and to serve others. We must not forget those lessons when our situations are no longer dire. We need to share such lessons with our families, colleagues, and others. Using what we learned from the pit, we should help others who are undergoing a similar challenge. In the case of Joseph, when he was a teenager, he was arrogant, making his brothers feel inferior before him. In explaining his dreams to them, he aggravated them.

Even when his brothers asked him if he was saying that he was superior to them, he never refuted the statement or apologized to his brothers. This was one of the contributing factors to his brothers' hatred for him and ultimately deciding to exile him. During his trials, he learned to be humble, selfless, and caring. The legacy here is that what matters is not the pit we find ourselves in, but what we learn while there, and what we are able to do with it.

In our lives, God allows certain things to happen to us for His purpose. We should accept such challenges without complaining. In the case of Joseph, God allowed his brothers to sell him in Egypt, so he could save his family and the world alike. Imagine if Joseph had constantly complained during his trials. Perhaps, he would missed out on the dreams God had in stock for him.

As my father always said, a lack of forgiveness makes us a prisoner to hatred. When we refuse to forgive, we hurt ourselves. We keep thinking about the event and continue to rehearse the scenario that led to the event. By so doing, we keep inducing pain on ourselves. We forget to realize that Jesus has forgiven us many times. Every time we commit one sin or another and ask God to forgive us, He does. Since God forgives us, we should also forgive those who have offended us.

My father warned us-his children- against taking revenge when we are wronged. He advised that when we are betrayed, we should avoid retaliating. Joseph, despite what he was going through, never fought back. He had every reason to retaliate and defend himself, but he chose not to. He could have physically done something terrible to Potiphar, a man whom he served very well but who chose to punish him wrongly. If Joseph was incapable of retaliating physically to Potiphar and his wife, he could have prayed to God to fight for him, but he did not do so. As humans, however, we sometimes tend to be very upset and try to take revenge. God will not bless us if we respond to evil with evil. Instead, He will bless us if we respond to evil with good. This is why in Romans 12:19, it says, "Do not take revenge, my dear friends, but leave room for God's wrath, for it is written: 'It is mine to avenge; I will repay,' says the Lord.

In a nutshell, we need to forgive those who have wronged us, so we, too, can be forgiven, because forgiveness is freedom—just as my father always preached.

CHAPTER 8

CHERISH YOUR FAMILY

Good memories flooded my mind as I stood in front of the altar with my five sisters, ready to sing our father's favorite song during his memorial service in 2017. At Saint Mary's Catholic Church in Obite community, his body lay in state while thousands of sympathizers listened to the memorial service, paying him their last respects.

Two weeks before the event, the entire community had gathered to plan his funeral ceremony. It was customary for the community to arrange this event, because my father died as an elder and a fulfilled man. Instead of purchasing one or two cattle to feed the guests at the funeral event, the family purchased ten cattle.

During the funeral planning meeting, the community leaders divided the funeral responsibilities among his children. Besides providing drinks, money, and other items, each member of the family was tasked with specific responsibilities.

Perpetua Anaele

My oldest sister, Kate, being the first daughter, was asked to purchase a bull and a beautiful casket, befitting our father's status as an accomplished elder. She was also asked to provide food, drinks, and money for all the unmarried women in the community to seek their approval to bury our father.

Sister Ange, the second daughter, was asked to purchase a bull, to take care of the mortuary bill, and to provide an ambulance for the casket transportation.

Bro. Polly, being the first son, was tasked with purchasing a bull and arranging all the gunshots for the event. He was also asked to provide some money and drinks to my father's maternal people in Umuoye to seek their approval to bury our father.

My next older sister, Beth, was asked to buy a bull, decorate the place where my father would lie in state, and handle all canopies and chairs for the event.

I was asked to buy a bull, repaint my father's house, and assist Bro. Polly with whatever tasks he was assigned to do.

My next younger sister, Juliet, was asked to buy a bull and assist Sister Kate with her responsibilities.

Ebere, my youngest sister, was asked to buy a bull and support Sister Ange with her responsibilities.

My brother Emeka, the second son, was tasked with purchasing a bull and paying for the posters, the pamphlets, and media materials for the event.

Nothing Left Undone

The last of our nine siblings, Iheanyi, was asked to support Beth with her responsibilities.

At the funeral planning meeting, two extended family members, Silvanus and Felix, volunteered to donate a bull each, making up the total of ten cattle for the event. Some extended family members and friends pledged different things, such as goats, chicken, drinks, money, and other things needed during the burial ceremony. The interment ceremony was, indeed, a community effort, reinforcing the important role community plays in helping one another at the point of need.

On Friday, July 7, 2017, my family began my father's funeral event. It was well organized and attended by many people whose lives my father had one way or another positively touched. It was a day and night of tribute from my father's friends, church members, family, and others. My father's compound that day was filled with so many people that the road had to be closed to prevent cars from coming to the area. Some activities included a live traditional music band and an outstanding Saint Mary's Catholic Church-organized Service of Songs. Three Catholic priests conducted the tribute service that night while I did the Bible reading. The Obite Catholic Choir celebrated my father through singing of familiar worship songs. It was a very memorable event.

The next day, Saturday, July 8, a procession of people, including musicians, brought my father's casket home from the mortuary, announced by gunshots. Later, the procession took his casket to his maternal family in Umuoye for public viewing. Once the viewing there was over, they brought his casket back to his house in Obite for the viewing. After the community viewing, the procession took his casket to Saint Mary's Catholic Church for the memorial service.

The weather that day was great, accompanied by comfortable temperature and a blue sky. The Catholic Church was filled with so many people that some had to stay outside the church. It was like a wedding banquet, with heaven welcoming our father home.

Later, during the memorial service, my sisters and I were asked to sing a farewell song to our father. As we began to sing "Just as I Am," I could picture my father singing the song with us. It was a song that meant so much to him, reminding him of the forgiving power of God. I smiled as we began to sing the song, taking a look at his beautiful casket and thanking God for the wonderful life he had lived:

> *Just as I am, without one plea*
> *But that Thy blood was shed for me,*
> *And that Thou bid'st me come to Thee,*
> *O Lamb of God, I come, I come!*

After singing the song, we sat down, and I gently opened the funeral event booklet and quietly read some emotional eulogies from his family members, friends, and others whose lives he had positively touched.

The funeral event, including the memorial service, is posted on YouTube, titled "Elder Lawrence Nwalozie Nwosu," and below are eulogies from my children, my husband, and me:

Tribute to our Grandpa

The greatest gift we received last Christmas was the opportunity to meet our families, especially you, our grandpa, after several years apart. Meeting you, though momentarily, was beyond amazing, and we are very thankful for that. Half of us did not even recognize you due to being away for so long. But for what we've lacked in conversation with you, our mother has filled with story after story of your bravery, compassion, and steadfast grip to the truth.

Not many men use their God-given ability, love, and vigor to bring so many people together, but luckily, Grandpa, you were one of the few. Through your love for your wife, our grandma, and your children, you developed a strongly linked family bond that continues to grow through each one of them, including us. We see you in the eyes and in the giving hearts of our aunts and uncles, and their successes today are testaments to your teachings and guidance. In our mother, Grandpa, you are not forgotten. She has instilled in us your hard work and your love for God and humanity. Consequently, any successes we, your grandchildren, experience in life are equally due to your many sacrifices.

— Jamal, Beverly, Hollys, and Rejoice

Perpetua Anaele

A Father's Love—Eulogy for My Father-in-Law

What can compare to a father's love?
My dear father-in-law, your love for me was impeccable.
On April 30, 1994, you proclaimed before the world,
"From today, Fyne is my son."
Your heart was big enough to take me in and welcome me like a son.
So, here I am to bid you farewell like a father.
But you also brought about the love between me and my wife.
You named her after your dear sister, Nwafor,
And molded her into the person she is today.
I see you in her. I see you in me.
I loved you until death.
So shall I love and protect her until death.
Ceaselessly, you asked that I bring my children home to you.
I did not see the sign that you were ready to leave us.
But patiently you waited till last December and bestowed on them grandpa's blessing.
Your love for God drew me in.
Your humility engulfed my heart.
Your courage pulled me in.

Your wisdom guided me.
Your support emboldened me.
Your compassion secured me in.
Your life rarely strayed from the lessons you taught.
Therefore, *forgotten* is a word you will never be.
Sir Nwosu, my in-law, my elder and mentor, go in peace and make way for us in heaven.

—Dr. Sabinus Fyne Anaele

My Father, My Idol

Dear Papa,

I can hardly believe it that you are no more; that I can't speak to you on the phone anymore or even see you when next I visit. I still can't believe that your laughter and jokes have all ceased and that your calm nature is no more.

No amount of words can explain what you meant to me, or what your passing has caused and will continue to cause me. From an early age, Papa, you planted in me the seeds of faith, love, and respect, showering me with an unconditional affection, and teaching me valuable life lessons that have carried me through to this day. I am grateful.

You were a dedicated and hardworking man with a big heart and unlimited compassion. You gave freely, often denying yourself some necessities so others could be satisfied. You selflessly made my welfare and that of my siblings your top priority, working hard each day, often juggling between being a father, a farmer, and a teacher, to ensure your children received the best in life. And for that, I am grateful.

Being guided by your longstanding conviction that when a woman is educated, her family prospers, and when her family prospers, the entire community benefits, you recognized early on the importance of female education and made it mandatory that not only my brothers became educated but my sisters and I as well. This is even more striking given that at that time the society considered female education trivial and encouraged early marriage. Instead of satisfying the status quo, you extraordinarily empowered us, your daughters, to cultivate a lifelong love of learning. Today, your investment has paid off, as all of your children are educated and are continuing your legacy of giving back to the society. I am grateful.

How about your integrity and loyalty, Papa? You sacrificed your life to doing good to others without expecting anything in return. You stood fast to what you believed in and courageously defended the weak even when doing so caused you some pain.

Nothing Left Undone

Your excellence of work as a missionary interpreter and a headmaster outstandingly exemplified your loyalty to the society. And for that, I am grateful.

Your simple approach to life is remarkable, and your zeal for a peaceful world is astonishing, demonstrating an amazing example of how fathers should be. You were such a peaceful man that even at the point of death, your last wish and word was peace, peace, and peace. I am grateful.

Despite all those achievements and more, you were never arrogant, and you never wavered in your faith in God, reminding me that the most important thing in life is my spiritual inheritance. You evidently lived a model life that Paul in Colossians 3:12 urged all Christians to live: a life clothed "with compassion, kindness, humility, gentleness, and patience."

Now that you are with God, the footprint of freedom you left behind in this world will endure forever, and I wish to continue such a fabulous legacy. Rest in peace, Papa, until we meet again.

Love,

Your lovely daughter,

Perpetua

Perpetua Anaele

After the funeral ceremony on Saturday, July 8, our family, along with our guests, organized a Thanksgiving service for our father at the same church on Sunday, July 9. The event was also well attended and offered an opportunity for our family and friends to give a special thanksgiving to God for the life our father had lived in this world. It was also an opportunity for our family to thank everyone who helped to make the funeral ceremony a success.

One of the greatest gifts God gave me through my father was our family. My father had a vision of his ideal family—a Christian family united by the love of God—and he worked so hard to achieve his vision. He did all he could to make sure he met our needs, providing us care and support, ranging from shelter, food, clothing, protection, and education, to love.

My father also equipped us with the skills necessary for our survival in the world. He taught us how to be hardworking, persistent, resilient, determined, visionary, content, thankful, caring, forgiving, humble, and respectful, among other things. He was a wonderful father who loved his family unconditionally. He gave us his all, so that we could survive and become meaningful members of society. He treasured each and every member of the family.

My father hustled day and night to keep food on the table for his family. From hunting to fishing, my father gave us enough to eat in those days. Whenever he did not have the time to hunt, he would buy meat from vendors. In fact, all the meat vendors in the village in those days knew the type and quantity of meat our family needed, and they ensured

Nothing Left Undone

they provided them for us. It was that important a family tradition that we could not cook any food without meat or fish.

I remember looking forward to my father arriving from his teaching station every day with carrots, garden eggs, groundnuts, boiled eggs, oranges, beef, or fish. Even when he visited his friends in the village, he would often come home with food for the family to share. No matter how small the food was, he would ask that we share it equally. It is a testament to my father's loving care that my siblings and I were often disappointed any day he did not return home from his teaching engagement.

On weekends, my father would go to the farm to harvest some yam tubers. At times, we would ask him to stay home and relax, but he would refuse, because he enjoyed taking care of his family.

Besides providing food for the family, my father made sure his children had decent rooms in his house. He built a ten bedroom house, which was sizeable for us. The girls stayed in separate rooms from the boys. If there was an issue, such as a broken window or door, he would immediately bring someone to fix the problem.

My father ensured we had nice clothes to wear, especially to church every Sunday. On Sundays, after each person is done dressing up in his or her Sunday best, my father would begin riding everyone on his motorcycle to church. I normally sat at the back, crushed in between two other sisters and holding the Bible while one person sat at the gas tank. Carefully, he would ride his motorcycle, waving and greeting other churchgoers along the way. On meeting a crowd of churchgoers blocking the road, he would gently tap the horn on his motorcycle, signaling them to make way for us. At church, we would take our usual front spot at the pew, awaiting our father to bring the rest of our family members. At the end of service, he would go the same route, dropping us all back home.

On Christmas, New Year's, and Easter holidays, my father would buy my sisters and me lovely colorful dresses, with matching earrings, necklaces, watches, sunglasses, shoes, and hats. Although the watches, eyeglasses, and shoes were made of plastic, we did not care. They were simply beautiful, and that was what mattered to us. We would differentiate who owned what by the colors of the accessories.

Before purchasing us the dresses and shoes at the market, he would measure our feet with broomsticks and our heights with rope to determine the sizes of our shoes and dresses. By so doing, he never bought us any dresses or shoes that were not our sizes. I can still recall the colors of one of my Christmas dresses and the accessories—a multicolored dress, with red shoes, a red hat, a red watch, and red sunglasses. I remember dancing and displaying my beautiful Christmas outfit to my friends.

For the boys, he would buy different colors of suits and matching shoes, sunglasses, ties, and watches. From the way they laughed after dressing up, I could tell that they, too, liked their Christmas presents.

When I was growing up, my family did many things in unison. For example, we completed our house chores together, ate together, and worshipped God together. On special holidays, like Christmas and New Year's, we would gather very early—around five o'clock—in my father's living room to sing, pray, and worship God until eight o'clock.

For Christmas, while we were gathered, my father would recite the biblical story of the birth of Jesus Christ and the visit of the Magi, along with their gifts. We would rehearse the familiar story about the birth of Jesus. It was a practice I adored so much that I began doing the same for my family in the United States, asking each of my family members what Christmas means for him or her. During Easter holidays, we did the same thing with my father, focusing on the biblical story of the crucifixion of Jesus Christ.

Every November 22 to 28, Obite community celebrated its Thanksgiving event, which was equivalent to the American Thanksgiving holiday. The event was a unique period of sharing, rejoicing, giving, and celebrating. It was forbidden to work during those days, as various festivities were attended to. Everyone dressed in his or her best outfit and visited others in celebration of life. I don't know if the Thanksgiving event still takes place today. In those days, my father would provide us and our guests a surplus amount of food and drinks and would ensure that the event was a success.

My father's love for his family was, indisputably, unshakable. He instilled in us the spirit of unity, encouraging us to be there for each other through life's ups and downs. We did everything in love and still do. When one person celebrates, we celebrate, and when one person mourns, we all mourn.

In 2013, when my sister Ebere got married, the entire family was around. After a successful traditional marriage in the community, the family was exhausted. Around five o'clock the following morning, my father, despite his old age, woke everyone up, informing us that he would like us to thank God for a successful marriage. We all then gathered in his living room and began to sing and praise God as we did in those old years. After a short prayer, he began advising us.

"My children," he said, "always look after each other. If you are eating and your brother or sister has nothing to eat, share. As you know, it is very easy to break a broomstick but very difficult for a bundle of broomsticks to be broken. In other words, together we stand, but divided we fall. Love yourselves, and do not allow worldly issues to cause a rift between you. Learn to support one another, and encourage each other. You should be concerned for the welfare of your siblings. Learn to accept each other's differences and encourage one another's talents. No matter what, you need each other, as a tree cannot make a forest …"

As he continued to advise us, I became very emotional, and Ebere then remarked that if there was anything called reincarnation, she would like to have the same parents and siblings in her next world. She could not be more right. My family was the best family anyone could ever ask for—thanks to my parents.

It is true that no family is perfect, but I admire the fact that our parents unified us to resolve whatever issue we had amicably. We were raised not to bear protracted grudges against each other. When we have issues with one another, we resolve them as soon as possible. For those we mistakenly offend, we were raised to apologize immediately and to forgive.

Some time ago, I had a discussion with my mother on whose idea—hers or my father's— it was to have such a good Christian home. She explained that she would give most of the credit to my father. She added that she was only seventeen years old when my father proposed to and married her. During that time, my father was already interpreting to the white missionary priests in a Catholic church, and she happened to be a member of the Legion of Mary in that church. At that time, she only had a Standard Five education and ended up completing Standard Six in my father's village in 1959, getting married to him the same year. In those days, they were taught that if they kept malice with anyone longer than two hours, they had already committed a sin.

"Having that kind of upbringing," she said, "it was difficult for us not to forgive each other."

My father did his best to protect each and every member of his family. When going to the farm, he would accompany and assist us, and every night after dinner, he was always the last to go to bed. He would always remind us to lock our windows and doors before falling asleep.

Perpetua Anaele

One night, in the village, there was a full moon, and the sky was covered with beautiful stars. The heat was excruciating. Juliet and I were sharing one room, so that night, we left the windows open in order to get some fresh air. Before going to bed, my father had reminded us—as he did every night—to close and lock the door and windows, and we promised him we would. But after tossing and rolling on the bed, we began to sleep, forgetting to lock the windows.

Suddenly, something began to crawl on my bed. At first, I thought I was dreaming, but when I woke up, I noticed that something was, indeed, touching my body. I jumped up, screaming and letting Juliet know that there was a snake in the room. She and I ran out of the room, shouting "Snake, snake, snake!" We knocked on our father's door, asking him to open it for us.

My father then ran out of his room with a knife, shouting, "Where is the snake?"

Trembling, we responded, "In our room."

He went to our room, looking for the snake. Later, he came out and told us that the snake had gone, and that we should go back to bed. Very terrified, Juliet and I refused to go back to our room, pleading that he should allow us to share his bed with him and our mother that night. He kept saying, "Did you remember to close and lock the windows and the door like I asked you to?"

But we said, "No, Papa."

Nothing Left Undone

He then said, "Well, it is not happening. You cannot sleep with us tonight because the bed is not enough for four people. Go back to your room and sleep."

As he was still talking, Juliet and I ran to his room and threw ourselves down on his bed, laughing. He tried in vain to make us leave. That night, we all slept on the same bed.

In the morning, my mother began joking and laughing over the incident. When I asked her why she was laughing, she said, "Your father was the snake that kept you up last night."

Walking closer to her in disbelief, I said, "Nma, what exactly are you saying?"

Laughing, she said, "Your father staged everything. There was no snake in your room. He did what he did because on several occasions, he has asked you and Juliet to lock the door and windows, but you never remembered to. Perhaps after he's done this, you won't forget to lock your door and windows." She continued to laugh.

I was dumbfounded. I can still remember how loud my father was laughing that morning and praising himself for coming up with such a brilliant plan to scare us. Although I was unhappy about what he did, the incident taught me that he cared, and since that day, I never left the windows or the door open.

My father's act of love was unquestionable. He showered us with so much love that there was no need for us to look for love elsewhere. Every time our hair grew, he would use his scissors and meticulously trim our hair. He knew what hairstyle to give the girls and the style to give the boys. When we outgrew our school uniforms, he was the first one to notice, and he got us new ones. If our shoes were worn out, he would get us new shoes; the list goes on and on. He had pet names for all of us and a peculiar way of calling us each name with sincere love. Mine was Adanem Nwafor. He would call me the name with much love that I felt very special and would shyly respond, "Papamyer."

He never dyed his gray hair, so once or twice a week, after I finished the family chores, he would ask me to begin removing some gray hair from his head. This normally took about an hour, but he made it so interesting that I did not worry about how long it took me to help him. He would tell me story after story.

On one such day, he told me that he had named me after his oldest sister, Nwafor, who was precious to him. He said that the sister cared a great deal for him but passed away at a time when he did not have the means to repay her. For that reason, every time he saw me, I reminded him of that woman, and he had to shower me with the love he had for her. I enjoyed hearing stories from my father, and we had a very affectionate relationship until his death in 2017.

My father never practiced favoritism. The same way he loved me was the same way he loved every member of the family. Even when he was so old, he could still recognize our voices on the phone when we called him. The moment I called on the phone, he would say, "Perpetua, how are you?" That made me so happy. That was why it pained me so much a day before he passed away when he could no longer recognize my voice or perhaps he could, but he did not want to utter a word.

My father always protected our family during the most trying times of our lives. My mother, in 2020, told me the important role my father played in keeping the family together and protected during the Nigeria-Biafra Civil War, which took place from 1967 to 1970.

According to her, even though the war started in 1967, our family did not move to Mbaise, Imo State, until late 1969 when the Nigerians fighting the Biafrans were closer to Obite community. My parents had five children then, and I was not yet born. My mother explained that in early 1969, my father took his family to Mbaise. They walked several miles, at times, sleeping in the bush. My father, somehow, provided food for all, often helping my mother carry their tired children.

On arriving at Mbaise, my father displayed his strong leadership skill and was soon made a leader of the refugees in his camp. With this responsibility, he was allocated food, medicine, clothes, and other items to distribute to the rest of the internally displaced persons at the camp. He discharged his duties painstakingly and became very popular at the camp. Although malnutrition was a problem during the war, the refugees who were under my father's care were well fed. My father also helped protect everyone at the camp. He maintained a good relationship with the Mbaise family, who supported our family during the war. He was respected and referred to as Sir Nwosu, the teacher.

Perpetua Anaele

When the war ended in 1970, my father brought everyone safely back home and continued to help the returnees adjust to their normal lives in Obite. My mother also pointed out that her parents and siblings had all stayed with her in my father's house in Obite, because the bridge connecting her village—Umuaturu, in Etche, Rivers State—was destroyed by the Nigerian soldiers.

While in Obite, my father provided food, shelter, and medicine to everyone in his family. Months later, when the bridge at Umuature was repaired, my mother's relatives returned to their village. She added that throughout the time that her relatives lived with them, there was no issues with my father whatsoever. She also informed me that her son, Vanacious, had died while her relatives were in Obite, and that her relatives' presence helped her recover quickly from the loss. According to her, my sister, Beth, was only one-year-old then.

My father was very supportive of us, his children. He made us dream big dreams of succeeding in life. He made sure all of his nine children were educated. He kept telling us about the importance of education and ensured we understood and pursued it as a means of survival. This was even more remarkable, considering that he had mainly girls, and in those days, girls were not given equal treatment to boys. In our situation, however, he made sure every one of us took advantage of being educated. At times, when he was not paid on time, he would ask us to harvest his cassava tubers, sell them, and use the proceeds to pay our school fees.

Mr. Lawrence Nwosu did not send us to school and simply leave us there. He ensured we each received quality education. For example, I began attending the secondary school in Obite when I was young. Later, when most of the teachers had left the school, my father changed institution for me to Etche Girls' Secondary School, Umuola Etche, Rivers State. It was an all-girls boarding school, which meant that my father had to pay the boarding fees, transportation, and school fees as opposed to the day school in my village, where he only paid my school fees.

He gave every member of the family the same opportunity. My mother, for example, completed her education while married to my father. Sister Ange went to a boarding school in Ogoni in Niger Delta, Rivers State; Beth went to the same boarding school that I went to in Umuola; Bro. Polly attended a school in Eberi, Rivers State; Iheanyi went to County Grammar School, Ikwerre Etche, Rivers State; and so on and so forth.

My father never used his meager salary to buy a car. Instead, he invested it in us. He knew that since he had brought us into this world, it was his responsibility to take care of us regardless. He did that without grumbling. Even in his old age, he continued to take care of us and remind us to love each other.

It is disheartening that today some parents abandon the education of their children. They leave the cost of training of their children to others, and if others are incapable of training those children, they will be uneducated. My father inculcated in us moral values, such as humility, honesty, love, and respect. He made sure we were our brother's keeper. He valued us as a people and never allowed others to mistreat us.

One day, when I arrived at school late in Obite, one of the teachers flogged me so hard that he broke a finger on my right hand. My father was, understandably, upset. He asked me to jump on his motorcycle, and I did. He took me to the teacher and threatened to report him to his supervisor if he did not stop carrying out such a harsh punishment. The teacher fell on his knees, pleading with him and promising that he would never flog me or any student again. Sure enough, until that teacher left Obite, he never laid a hand on me or on any student.

My father was, indeed, a phenomenal man who took his fatherly responsibilities seriously, raising a wonderful family. I am so proud to be his daughter and thank God for such great blessings my father had given his family.

CHAPTER 9

LOVE IS THE GREATEST OF ALL GIFTS

If I speak in the tongues of men or of angels, but do not have love, I am only a resounding gong or a clanging cymbal. If I have the gift of prophecy and can fathom all mysteries and all knowledge, and if I have a faith that can move mountains, but do not have love, I am nothing. If I give all I possess to the poor and give over my body to hardship that I may boast, but do not have love, I gain nothing. Love is patient, love is kind. It does not envy, it does not boast, it is not proud. It does not dishonor others, it is not self-seeking, it is not easily angered, it keeps no record of wrongs. Love does not delight in evil but rejoices with the truth. It always protects, always trusts, always hopes, always perseveres. Love never fails. But where there are prophecies, they will cease; where there are tongues, they will be stilled; where there is knowledge, it will pass away. —1 Corinthians 13:1–8

Years ago, when I was about fifteen, I had just returned from boarding school, shivering with a high temperature. I had lost weight and could neither eat any food nor drink water. Being too tired to walk, I lay on the bed, covered with sweat. Luckily, my father had just returned from his teaching station. On seeing my situation, he quickly asked, "Perpetua, what's going on? When did you return? Oh, my goodness. You have lost a lot of weight."

Weakly, I responded, "This afternoon, Papa. I'm really sick. I think I have malaria."

Holding my hands and pulling me up from the bed, he said, "Try and get up. I will take you to the clinic right away. Have you eaten something?"

"No, Papa, I'm not hungry."

As he helped me onto his motorcycle, he asked, "Do you want someone to sit behind and hold you? I really don't want you to fall down."

Shaking and covered with sweat, I said, "No, Papa, I will be fine. Let's go."

As he started his motorcycle to leave, he asked me to grasp him firmly around the waist to keep from falling. I did. He gently rode the motorcycle, avoiding potholes and frequently asking if I was okay.

We arrived at the clinic thirty minutes later, and he immediately alerted the doctor of my situation, asking him to take care of me right away. Suspecting my illness to be malaria, the doctor admitted me and began running some tests and administering his treatment regimen. While at the clinic, my father sat at my bedside, holding my hands and pleading with me to get well soon. He then rubbed a wet cloth all over my body to cool down my temperature. After receiving the initial treatment from the doctor, I began to sleep. When I woke up six hours later, my father was still at my bedside, watching over me like a guardian angel. Out of pity, I asked, "Papa, are you still here? It's dark outside."

"Yes, my daughter. How are you feeling now?"

Sitting on the bed, I responded, "I think I'm a bit better. Thank you. You've been here for a long time. The nurse will take care of me. Please go home."

"You are my priority," he responded. "I won't go home until I'm sure you will be fine."

The nurse then came in and brought some food for me to eat. "This is for you," she said. "Try and eat something." She then left the room, but the smell of the food—fried rice and chicken—nauseated me. I tried not to show this, however.

"Eat while the food is still hot, my daughter."

"No, Papa. I'm not hungry. When I am, I will eat."

"And when will that be, my daughter? You are very weak because you haven't eaten anything. Force yourself to eat a little rice, and you will be fine."

Without waiting to hear my response, he scooped some rice on the spoon and began to feed me. "Open your mouth and eat, my daughter. Just try."

I did. He waited until I chewed and swallowed the rice before bringing another spoon of rice. "Open."

I did.

"You are doing a good job. If you continue this way, you will get better in no time and go home soon, my daughter."

"Thank you, Papa."

He waited again until I swallowed the rice before bringing forth another spoonful. Just as he was giving me a third spoon, I threw up. He quickly dropped the spoon and held me while I continued to throw up. With one hand massaging my chest and the other holding my back, he said, "Take it easy; you will be fine."

After throwing up, I weakly lay back on the bed while my father contacted the nurse to bring him a bucket of water, a clean towel, and some clothes. She did, and my father began to give me a bed bath. After cleaning me up, he took some lotion from my bag, rubbed me some, and dressed me up with the clothes the nurse had given him. Later, I drifted off to sleep, and he went home.

In the morning, he returned to the clinic to continue his care and support. Throughout the three days I spent there, my father was present most of the time, taking care of me and keeping me company. After my discharge from the clinic, my father took me home and helped me recuperate. He prepared local medicine for me in addition to the regular medicine I had received from the doctor and ensured that I took them as prescribed. Once I fully recovered, my father bought me some provisions and rode me back to school on his motorcycle. Yes, that was my father—a compassionate and loving man!

My father's outpouring of love extended beyond the family. He would ask us, his children, to share some food with orphans and widows, especially during Christmas and New Year's celebrations. Women, who had issues with their husbands, would come to him for financial assistance, and he would help them.

Without a doubt, my father left the legacy that love is the greatest of all gifts. Throughout his life, he showed his family and others what true love actually meant. In loving us, he never provoked us. He knew each of his children very well and what worked and what didn't. He took the message of Proverbs 22:6 seriously: "Start children off on the way they should go, and even when they are old they will not turn from it." He created time for his family despite how busy he was. He never showed any sign of favoritism.

My father was very patient with us. His patience could be likened to that of the gardener in the Parable of the Barren Fig Tree in the Bible. There, Jesus speaks about a certain man who had a fig tree in his yard and for three years, the tree had not borne any fruit. He then asked the man who took care of the vineyard to cut down the tree since it had not borne any fruit after three years and was occupying the ground. But the man pleaded, "Leave it alone for one more year, and I'll dig around it and fertilize it. If it bears fruit next year, fine! If not, then cut it down" (Luke 13:6–9).

Perpetua Anaele

My father had his family's goodwill in mind and was patient while helping us-his children- to succeed. I remember how patient he was with me years ago when I took my first West African Senior School Certificate Examination. In those days, my first examination results were canceled. It was absolutely normal for the results to be canceled then. The West African Examination Council (W.A.E.C.), the body responsible for administering the examinations, would often feel that there was some malpractice during the examination and would not release students' results. This meant that every student who took the examination, irrespective of the fact that the student never cheated, would be punished, because he or she happened to take the examination in a center where the alleged malpractice took place.

At times, out of eight subjects a student had written during the examination, W.A.E.C. would only release one or two subjects, making it difficult for that student to further his or her education. In other words, without the passing the remaining papers, the student would not enter into any university. In that situation, therefore, the student would have to take another examination, and if he or she happened to be enrolled in a malpractice center, the results would still be canceled.

A very intelligent friend of mine gave up on education as her results were constantly canceled. Her situation was bad, because she was an orphan who literally relied on relatives to register for those examinations. In her third attempt to register, her relatives could no longer afford the expenses. Therefore, she borrowed some money from her friends to register for it. Unfortunately, after she had spent the money and taken the examination, W.A.E.C. still canceled her results. She has never furthered her education as a result.

In my situation, after taking my first examination, W.A.E.C. only released five subjects, withholding my English and Mathematics. I performed exceptionally well on the ones W.A.E.C. released, but that was not enough for me to enter any university in Nigeria. I don't know if it is still the case today, but in those days, a student must pass English and Mathematics to be admitted into a university in Nigeria.

On encountering this adversity, I was distraught, but my father was patient with me and encouraged me to retake the examination. For me to retake the test, I had to research different centers and hope none of the centers would be involved in malpractice. This was a daunting task since I could not predict what would happen on the examination day. My father took it upon himself to join me in researching the issue. We finally figured out a school where malpractice was supposedly rare. He registered and provided me with some resources to get me prepared for the examination. Later, when my results were released, I passed all my subjects —thanks to my father.

As an adult, I had a great time with my father. In 2003, when he visited my family in Maryland, he joined me in Washington, D.C. to attend my husband's Swearing-in Ceremony as a United States Foreign Service Officer.

Perpetua Anaele

My Father – Middle- Attending my Husband's United States Foreign Service Officer Swearing-in Ceremony, Washington, D.C., August, 2003

Nothing Left Undone

My Father and I in Washington, D.C., August, 2003

We went to the event that day by train. As that was his first time being on the train, my father kept asking me where the railroad engineer was, and why the train would be going underground. Being mesmerized with the beauty of the United States, he kept admiring the tall architectural designs, as well as the roads in Washington, D.C.

During his visit, my father joined me to attend a Catholic Mass at the Basilica of the National Shrine of the Immaculate

Perpetua Anaele

Conception in Washington, D.C. He was astonished at the artistic design of the church.

The shrine is the largest Catholic Church in the country. It is located adjacent to the Catholic University of America and hosts several Masses for different organizations of the church. The church is simply magnificent, and visitors never get bored. Every corner of the church is beautifully decorated, welcoming everyone to view the designs. The ceiling is incredibly intricate with astonishing designs. Every now and then during Mass, my father would gaze up at and admire the ceiling.

After the service, we toured decorated corners of the church, meditated, and took some pictures. Being a Catholic, my father, undeniably, enjoyed his visit to the church.

My Father at Catholic University of America, Washington, D.C., 2003

Nothing Left Undone

My Father in Washington, D.C., 2003

My father never envied people who succeeded in his community. Instead, he rejoiced with them and made us—his children—realize that anyone who works hard deserves to reap from his or her hard work. He understood the dignity of work. Most of the people in my father's community who studied abroad became my father's friends due to his fatherly support and advice to them. They would often send him gifts, such as Christmas and New Year's greeting cards, and in each of those cards, they would write nice notes, thanking him for supporting them.

In the entire Obite community, everyone knows that my father was never proud; he was never arrogant. He was a calm man who only spoke when necessary, and when he did, his speech was full of wisdom. He never made any kind of boastful display. While having five of his children in the United States was a big deal to some, my father never portrayed himself as rich. He never changed from being the peaceful and loving father that he was. He never engaged in self-glory.

Yes, it is true that there is no perfect family. Whenever my mother or any of us mistakenly wronged my father, he would gently remind us about it, and when we apologized, he forgave us immediately. Throughout the time I lived with my parents, I never saw my father harm my mother or the two of them quarrel.

I had an interesting discussion with my mother years ago. I was discussing our upbringing with her and then asked, "Nma, throughout my childhood, I never saw you and Papam quarrelling. Do you mind sharing your secret with me?"

Smiling, she said, "Pepe, my daughter, we actually did quarrel."

Shocked, I asked, "You did? When? How come none of us, your children, knew about it?"

"Well, we did not quarrel in the presence of our children. When we got married, we had agreed that as a couple, no third party—not even our children—would hear us quarrel. In situations when we did quarrel, we did so privately."

This was amazing because, growing up, I often saw couples shouting and screaming at each other and fighting openly. In my family, however, there was nothing like that. Because my father never openly quarreled with my mother, I did not see him counting grievances against her.

My father expressed his love for humanity and God in different ways. He would often say, "In anything you do, my children, do it to please God. If you cook, cook to please God. If you study, study to please God. If you clean the house, do so to please God."

As an adult, I have been applying this legacy in everything I do. While at work, I put in my best, knowing that I am doing it for God. Doing so motivates me to be successful despite the challenges along the way.

For those who had misfortunes in the community, my father would mourn with them. He would give them words of inspiration, bringing them out of their mood quickly. The average person in the village was important to my father. He loved his in-laws passionately and talked highly of them. He had a great relationship with his relatives and treated them like family. Everyone in the community called him

Perpetua Anaele

Sir Nwosu due to his interest in education and counseling techniques. He was well respected because of what he represented.

My family may not have been a perfect one, but I am happy that God made me a part of it. Colossians 3:18–21 says "Wives, submit yourselves to your husbands, as is fitting in the Lord. Husbands, love your wives and do not be harsh with them. Children, obey your parents in everything, for this pleases the Lord. Fathers, do not [provoke] your children, or they will become discouraged."

My father exemplified the Bible quotation above, setting up our family such that everyone knew what was expected of him or her. He was not selfish. My father gave his all to those who needed it.

His love for my mother was impeccable. He knew that loving her showed that he loved himself as stated in Ephesians 5:28, "Husbands ought to love their wives as their own bodies. He who loves his wife loves himself."

My father gave my mother breathing space, which was necessary for her to showcase her talent. He never constrained her to be a housewife, unlike some husbands who feel that their wives are their properties and mistreat them.

Based on the lessons I learned from my father, a wife needs her husband's presence, his love, and his time. He needs to be there for her. A man should include his wife in his decisions and make her feel important and cherished.

Nothing Left Undone

My father never humiliated my mother. He believes that when a man adores his wife, he will bring out the best in her, and she will love him forever in return.

My father called my mother "Madam," and she referred to him as "Brother." When my mother visited my siblings and me in the United States years ago, we tried hard to keep her here, but she kept saying she would like to go back to the village to take care of our father. We could not understand why she could not stay a year in the U.S. without seeing our father. To us, she needed to get some rest; after all, our father had people in the village helping him. Meanwhile, our siblings in Nigeria continued to call us, asking us to send our mother back, as our father already needed his "Madam" and was asking her to come back. In the end, we had no choice but to let her return to her "Brother."

My Mother, Theresa Nwosu

Perpetua Anaele

My parents had a great relationship; no wonder they were the first people to be wedded in Obite community. It is a testament to my parents' exceptional loving care that some couples in the village had them as their godparents.

As a child of God, my father recognized that he and my mother were equal in dignity in God. My father always respected my mother, often seeking her advice on issues, taking time to listen to her, and taking her views on matters seriously. In return, my mother became a wonderful help to him, respecting him all the time. Many of the great decisions my father made, such as changing schools for his children and helping Obite community, he did so in consultation with my mother.

My mother was my father's anchor, making difficult sacrifices that made it possible for him to achieve his goals in life. For example, while my father was away studying, my mother took care of and protected the family. After my father completed his educational pursuits and began touring neighboring communities to teach, my mother also took care of the family in Obite, and at times, relocated with the family to my father's teaching station. She had to wait until my father completed his education before she began pursuing hers. My mother never criticized my father publicly. As a child, at times, I would not understand why my father made certain decisions, but my mother let me know that he had made the right decisions for me.

Although I never saw my parents holding hands like couples in the United States do, I could tell they were very much in love. They would tell jokes and laugh out loud from time to time. They both had a very good sense of humor. In difficult situations, they would downplay the issues so much that everyone in the family would all laugh, and the issues would become little or nonexistent.

My mother played a great role in enabling my father to achieve his dreams. She was a problem solver and had great attributes: she was loving, patient, kind, caring, hardworking, soft-spoken, and attentive. These qualities helped her to contribute positively to her children's upbringing. Like my father, my mother is my confidant. I feel comfortable letting her know of things bothering me, and when I do, she never judges me. She always gives me a listening ear.

My parents were attuned to each other and had similar goals. My mother told me how determined she was to be educated no matter what. After having ten children, she still pursued her teaching education and finally achieved her occupational dream. My mother complemented my father. As my father retired from teaching, my mother continued to support the family until she, too, later retired from teaching. She was always there for him-even at the final days of his life at the hospital, she was there for him.

As we were growing up, our parents made our home a place we felt comfortable returning to whenever we were away. Every time I went to the city, Port-Harcourt, I looked forward to coming home and enjoying the love of my family.

Our father made balanced decisions, reflecting God's will. He loved us, his children, so dearly, and we reciprocated this love by obeying him. He never overemphasized his authority as the head of the family. He encouraged us to ask him questions anytime or feel free to confide in him. He took his fatherly responsibilities seriously and never neglected any of his duties. He led by example and allowed everyone to follow in a respectful way. My father deserved our total obedience, because he represented our God on earth, had a wealth of knowledge, and wanted the best for us. In addition, he treated us as human beings, correcting us when we erred. As Proverbs 3:12 indicates, "For the Lord corrects those he loves, just as a father corrects a child in whom he delights," every time our father disciplined us for erring, we never took it personally.

One day, when I was about sixteen years old, I visited the village from the city during a Thanksgiving festive period. I went out with my sisters and my friends, and while we were there, one thing led to another, and I found myself drinking alcohol. As that was my first time drinking alcohol, I drank it as if it was juice. After that, I lost control of myself and began misbehaving. My sisters brought me home, covering my mouth to keep me from talking uncontrollably. On seeing my condition, my father was disappointed. He asked my sisters to take me to my room, and they did. I stayed there, saying all kinds of silly things until I fell asleep. In the morning, when I regained my senses, he called me privately and told me how disappointed he was in me. He made me promise him that I would never drink alcohol. I did, and it has been that way since then.

My father led by example, and there was no reason we could not have obeyed him. We respected him and brought him honor most times by our behavior in society. In many instances, people came to our parents and thanked them for raising wonderful children. That, undoubtedly, made them happy. We respected them, because they earned that respect by their actions.

Mr. Lawrence Nwosu lived a great life full of love and instilled in his children the legacy that love is the greatest gift of all, just as Saint Paul stated in 1 Corinthians 13:13, "And now these three remain: faith, hope and love. But the greatest of these is love."

I became a parent at a very early age, but the lessons I learned from my parents have been useful ever since. I relied heavily on what I learned from them, and I have so far never regretted it. As a parent, I have realized how difficult it is to raise children, which is a lifelong journey. When my children were sick, my husband and I had to be there for them. When they came home from school dejected, we had to console them. We made sure and still make sure we have family time together.

While living and working overseas, I have seen and heard people complaining about lack of social amenities. They blamed their elected officials for not developing their communities. The truth I learned from my father is that, even in developed countries, no government can provide every service for its people. Individuals, with humanitarian love, can do their best to assist one another. We have a responsibility to be our brother's keeper. We need to do something, no matter how little, to make the world a better place for all. Therefore, if a community lacks a school and someone is capable of constructing one, let that individual do so. The person will be helping to educate the children— future leaders— and also provide jobs for teachers. If there is a need for a community health center and an association is able to help, let it do so. That association will help save the lives of people while creating jobs for health care workers and others.

I have heard people say that when they are rich, they can help their communities. We do not need to be millionaires before helping out. God has given us various talents and expects us to use them as soon as possible to help others.

No doubt, many people across the world are generous. In America, for example, I have come across many generous people. While some were born to help, others became generous due to various circumstances. During this coronavirus pandemic, for example, I have heard of some people in America donating their food, time, money, and other resources to their neighbors and communities. Some give through their churches and work. They give without expecting any recognition. This is very outstanding. Please keep giving. From my experience, there is a reward in giving than receiving, and the more we give, the more we will receive.

In Rwanda, the government has instituted Umuganda, which is a Kinyarwandan word for "coming together in common purpose to achieve an outcome." It is a day of volunteerism and takes place on the last Saturday of every month. There, men and women come out to clean up the country, plant trees, and decorate their communities. No wonder the city of Kigali is spotless, the cleanest city in East Africa.

My father constantly reminded me that we have come into this world to help others and should be happy to discharge that duty to our struggling brothers and sisters. He urged his children to render a helping hand to our underprivileged brothers and sisters and help lift them from poverty. He believed that when we bless others, we will be blessed.

I clearly concur that those who bless others will be blessed. When I immigrated to the United States many years ago, my sister Ebere, who was in Nigeria then, called me on the phone, saying, "Perpetua, you won't believe what's happening in our compound right now!"

I responded, "Fill me in, sis; what's going on?"

"There are many people gathered in our father's compound right now," she said. "Most of them are military officers."

Dropping the clothes I was folding, I asked, "Who are they, and what are they doing?"

"Well," she continued, "about half an hour ago, a van full of military officers drove past our compound while we were sitting under the tangerine tree. A few minutes later, we saw some military officers marching toward our compound with a villager in front of them. We were so scared, so we ran to the backyard of the house. They entered our compound and came to the backyard. As they arrived, one of them began asking if this was Mr. Lawrence Nwosu's house. As we were not sure who they were, we did not know whether to say yes or no. Then, the villager who brought them in said, 'Yes, it is.'

"One of the soldiers then asked to speak with Papam. I went to the house and brought Papam out, shivering. As Papam came out, the soldier, removing his cap, knelt down in front of him, and held Papam's hands as he greeted him. As this was happening, many people in the community gathered at our backyard to figure out what was going on. When he was greeting Papam, he introduced himself as one of the teachers who had lived in our house years ago. Apparently, after he had left our community, he had joined the military and is now a high ranking officer in the military. He thanked Papam for the care and support he had given him while he was living in our house. As he was greeting Papam, the other soldiers began to salute Papam with gunshots. Everyone was overjoyed. Some soldiers then returned to the van and brought out various gifts for Papam. Right now, they are in the compound, and the entertainment is fantastic. I'm sorry that you are missing this pleasant surprise, sis."

"Wow, this is great! Papam is lucky to be appreciated for his benevolence," I responded.

This incident clearly shows that sometimes, some people appreciate what others have done for them. It also shows that when we do good things to others, somehow, we will be rewarded.

Apple Co-founder, Steve Jobs, on his deathbed, recognized the importance of making the most out of life. He indicated

Nothing Left Undone

that despite how rich he was, he had little joy as he did not focus on the little things that mattered most in life. He added that the "[n}onstop pursuing of wealth will only turn a person into a twisted being, just like me. God gave us the senses to let us feel the love in everyone's heart, not the illusions brought about by wealth. The wealth I have won in my life I cannot bring with me. What I can bring is only the memories precipitated by love. That's the true riches which will follow you, accompany you, giving you strength and light to go on. Love can travel a thousand miles…"

Jobs advised that we treasure love for our family, love for our spouse, love for our friends, and, most importantly, treat ourselves well and cherish others. Steve Jobs, like my father, was right. When people love one another, great things happen. My father, through his life, showed that love wins no matter what.

CHAPTER 10

A PEACEFUL HEART IS A HEALTHY HEART

For many years, I maintained a folder labeled Peaceful Living. It was almost filled with quotations, articles, and illustrations on how I could live in peace with people. Recently, I went through the folder, trying to refresh my mind on the topic. As I was going through it, I realized that while much of the information was helpful, some did not make sense at all. I then began throwing away the unnecessary advice and reflecting on what was helpful.

Then, it occurred to me that while I had the folder over the years, I never actually used it to resolve any issues I had. I recalled some poor decisions I had made, which I could have avoided had I referred to the folder prior to making such decisions. My mind also drifted to my father, who never kept such a folder but somehow knew exactly how to live amicably with people. I then concluded that instead of keeping a folder without referring to it when necessary, it would be better for me to focus on my father's peaceful living legacy.

Mr. Nwosu was, indisputably, a peaceful man. Everyone in the community recognized that his peaceful nature was exceptional. He overlooked certain things in life and learned to accept things that were beyond his control. While an average person would be stressed out with issues of the day, my father never seemed to worry much about such matters.

From my experience with my father, he approached problems in a peculiar way. First, he sought to deliberate and understand exactly what the issues were by asking appropriate questions. Second, he took his time to understand how the issues affected everyone involved. Third, he seemed to meditate on the issues by remaining calm and holding on to his Catholic rosary. At times, when he was calm, I used to think that he did not care about the issue at hand, but I was wrong. That was when he was actually reflecting continuously on that issue.

He normally came back with a list of possible solutions to the problem. From the list, he would solicit the opinion of the family or stakeholders to ensure he was making the right decision. After weighing the pros and cons of each solution listed, my father would come up with the best answer to the problem at hand. Such a resolution seemed to always work. When he did not have control over issues, he normally prayed about them and let us know that there was nothing we could do. For such issues, he would recommend that we accept the situations as they were. He avoided dwelling on these issues, because that would not solve the problem.

As a believer in Jesus Christ, my father had peace in the midst of uncertainties, because he had the assurance of

Perpetua Anaele

God to take care of his needs. He refused to be chained to life's difficulties. He employed tactics, such as humor and serenity, to achieve his inner peace. From time to time, especially during difficult circumstances, my father would say something funny, and everyone would start laughing.

One day, he, Juliet, and I went to the farm to harvest some cassava tubers. We harvested a lot of cassava tubers, and it was getting so late that Juliet and I could not carry them all to the road where someone could pick them up. We needed one more person to assist us to bring the remaining cassava tubers to the road. We then asked our father to please carry them to keep us from having to return to the farm that late. He never said a word.

I then said, "Papa, please give us a helping hand by bringing the remaining cassava tubers. As you know, it's almost dark, and Juliet and I cannot come back to the farm this late to bring them."

Looking at me in a funny way, he responded, "Perpetua, I will help you." Lifting his hand toward me, he said, "Here, you can take my hand now; it's okay."

I looked at him, unsure of what he meant and asked, "Papa, what are you talking about?"

He responded, "I thought you wanted a helping hand; I am giving you my hand. You can have it now. It's okay. Go ahead and have it." We all started laughing, and he then said, "Just kidding, I can carry the remaining cassava tubers."

Nothing Left Undone

Another example of his numerous jokes was in 2003 when he visited my siblings and me in the United States. He told us that while he was on the plane heading to the United States, there was terrible turbulence. As that was his first time being on a plane for a long time, he was certainly scared each time it happened and could not understand why people were sleeping under such a turbulence. Then, as the turbulence recurred, he quietly prayed to God as follows:

"Dear God, please help me make it to America safely. I do not want any plane crash or any form of issue on this flight. After you lead me safely to see my children and then bring me back to Nigeria, if you ever see me step on any plane, ask me what am I doing there? In Jesus' name I pray. Amen!"

This was funny, and as a matter of fact, he never returned to America. Each time we asked him to visit us in the U.S., he would simply say, "Remember my prayer? God has done His own part by bringing me safely back to Nigeria. I need to do my part too. Otherwise, He will ask me, 'What are you doing on this plane?'" Yes, my father was that funny!

He never welcomed any violent situation; he was always preaching peace to everyone. For example, if someone from the community visited him, after asking that individual how he or she was doing, his next question was always, "Is there peace in the community?" I could not understand that, but everyone expected him to ask that question, and he always did.

Whenever my siblings and I called him on the phone, he would not conclude his conversation with us without asking if we were living in peace. He always followed that question by urging us to live in peace. I would say that among all the virtues my father inculcated in us, peaceful living was his favorite virtue. It was so important to him that hours before he passed away in 2017, he kept saying we must live in peace; that all he wanted was peace, peace, and peace.

My father's demeanor was a shining example in his community of a peaceful lifestyle. He lived a simple life without bothering himself or others. He never set any unrealistic expectations. He managed his schedules well, prioritizing as necessary. Instead of assuming too much responsibilities and not meeting a deadline, my father picked and chose what he wanted to accomplish. The rest, he delegated to us or to others to do.

He never indulged in unwanted material things. He considered such things unnecessary and, therefore, never sought them. For example, my father could have bought a car if he had wanted to, but that would have meant that some of his children would not have been educated and some of the family needs would not have been met. He recognized that buying the car with a meager salary was not the main issue, but maintaining that car was. With his salary, purchasing a car would have put much pressure on him and depleted his inner peace. To him, it was not worth the stress. Instead, he chose to purchase a motorcycle, which he easily maintained, and it served him well.

This was also true of his monogamous family structure. He did his research at a young age and found out that most polygamous families had family conflicts that threatened the family members' peace of mind. "There is no way a man can love his wives equally," he reasoned. "If a man favors one wife over his other wives, such an action will definitely be a problem." So, despite the pressure from his friends, family members, and others to marry another woman, my father refused to do so.

My father focused on what mattered most to him and by so doing, he derived an inner peace and joy. I have heard people talk about world peace from time to time, with tension rising in some nations as people protest and demand their rights and freedom from their elected leaders. In an effort to maintain peace, some security officials carry out violent attacks on protestors, who are anxious to recover their freedom and maintain their dignities.

Each year, on September 21, experts organize symposiums after symposiums to celebrate the International Day of Peace, deliberating on how people can live together in peace. The United Nations, in 2015, adopted seventeen Sustainable Development Goals (SDG), with the sixteenth being "Peace, Justice and Strong Institutions." Despite the world's call for peace, the world is still not at peace.

Some countries fight their citizens, and some ethnic groups rise up against others. Having lived in Rwanda for almost two years, I was constantly reminded of what could happen when people refuse to live in peace.

In 1994, the country witnessed a genocide, in which the two main ethnic groups—Hutu and Tutsi—brutally massacred their relatives. With an estimated 800,000 people, many

Perpetua Anaele

of them Tutsis, killed, it was one of the worst atrocities in human existence, giving rise to orphans and women infected with Human Immunodeficiency Virus.

It is even more appalling given that the two ethnic groups are similar in many ways—they speak the same language, follow the same traditions, and live close to each other. Due to a lack of peace, however, their major differences, such as the Tutsis being taller and thinner than the Hutus, were used as identifying marks, partly giving rise to the conflict.

Every year, in April, Rwanda commemorates those who died during the war while preaching peace and reconciliation to those alive. After witnessing the 2018 commemoration and hearing copiously about peace in families, I came to the conclusion that we cannot achieve world peace without first loving our families.

People embrace war, as if it is the only solution to the world's problems. If there is something we should learn from World War I and II, it is that war is never a solution. Despite the number of people killed and the weapons developed, people are still not at peace. From my knowledge, nobody is given an award for being a warlord. Rather, people who embrace peace as a solution to problems are recognized through Nobel Peace Prizes.

My father taught me that acquiring material wealth does not guarantee peace. I recently read about someone who bought a mansion through a loan in a very expensive neighborhood. She and her husband bought this house, because they wanted to compete with the Joneses. They actually could not afford

Nothing Left Undone

that type of house, but they bought it anyway to prove to their friends that they belonged to the same class. Sadly, they forgot to realize that their friends made more money than they did and could comfortably afford to live in such a big house. In their situation, however, they left their four kids at home, as they worked day and night to earn the income to pay their mortgage.

At home, due to the lack of parental presence, their children began spending hours watching violent movies on the television. The situation deteriorated to the point that the children started performing poorly at school. As a result, two of them became drug addicts, and the other two dropped out of high school. In addition, their parents could not afford to pay their mortgage. Consequently, the bank, their lender, took over their house. Unfortunately, the family now lives in a shelter, trying to make ends meet. In that type of situation, I ask myself, "Where then is the peace of mind?"

My father knew that the trick to achieving inner peace was cutting his coat according to his size. He was contented with what he had, and as for things he could not afford, he simply never bothered trying for them. He passed on this legacy to his children.

When I was growing up, I noticed that some people enjoyed quarrelling with others, but my father handled such issues with caution. He knew that making peace did not necessarily mean avoiding conflict. He honestly and courageously faced problems head on but in a civilized way.

Perpetua Anaele

Acknowledging that in problem-solving, delay could be dangerous, since a minor issue could take root and develop into a serious and irreparable one, my father dealt with issues as early as possible. Diplomatically, he handled each issue, practicing restraint, especially in controlling what he said. He knew there was power in the tongue, so he carefully selected his words, avoiding to incite a flammable situation. He recognized that in making peace, things may not go as planned, so he often prepared for the worst case scenario, being patient at all times.

As an adult, I have come to realize that my father could not have been a peaceful and happy man without believing in God. He had faith in his Creator, and his Creator saw him through. He understood that one of the gifts a Christian could derive for serving God was the gift of peace. In all issues he encountered, he invited God, and He gave him the wisdom necessary to discern right from wrong.

My father capitalized on what was important—serving God—and in return, Jesus Christ, being the Prince of Peace, granted him the mercy to draw from His peace and gift of reconciliation. Throughout his life, my father preached forgiveness and reconciliation. He enjoyed seeing people happy. In our family, he would often ask us to forgive one another and to live in peace. He refueled his peace of mind by creating time to worship his God. His faith in God was unshakable as evidenced by his beautiful songs to God, his humility, and his love for humanity.

My father understood that when we excessively worry, it can impact our physical and emotional health. He also recognized that our constant worrying is an evidence of our lack of faith in God. That was why he avoided worrying altogether. He embraced a peaceful state of mind, which granted him access to health, happiness, and peace.

It was always my father's wish that the world live in peace. Through his actions and life experiences, nothing mattered more to him than peaceful living. "When everyone understands the need to live in peace and harmony, the level of violence will be decreased," he often said.

My father had a glorious and peaceful exit. A day before he passed in 2017, my siblings who were surrounding his hospital bed said he was crying. I did some research on why people would cry prior to dying, and I found out that most times, they did so for their loved ones.

Sister Ange told me that as our father was crying, she asked him why he was doing so. He said he was crying because of us, confirming my research. She then told him that it was okay, and that he did not need to cry for us. She assured him that we would be all right, because he had done a great job raising us, and that there was nothing to be worried about. My father somehow later stopped crying.

Then, the night before he passed, he began calling on one of our relatives, Dominic. Dominic was in the same room with him, but he was sleeping at the time. Sister Ange woke Dominic up and told him that my father was trying to speak with him. My father then turned to Dominic and said, "I want peace, peace, and peace; I don't want any trouble at all." Dominic responded that there would be peace.

Perpetua Anaele

The day he passed—June 1, 2017—my father had asked Sister Ange to give him some food to eat. She did, and he ate very well—much to my sister's surprise and appreciation, because before that day, he had not been eating well.

After eating, he began to call out for Ebere, who was in the United States at the moment. He called her three times: "Ebere, Ebere, Ebere." After saying her name, he began to sleep peacefully while Sister Ange went outside the room to call Ebere on the phone, so she could speak with him. After getting Ebere on the line and informing her that our father would like to speak with her, Sister Ange returned to the room to give the phone to our father, but he was gone. What a beautiful and peaceful way to go!

Each time I reflect on my father's peaceful exit, I thank God for the life he had lived and wish I could live to his age and return to my Creator the same way. It was as if his Creator was waiting for him, and he needed to speak one more time with his loved ones.

This brings me to a story I heard years ago. A woman in one church was very sick. The pastors and other members of the church prayed for her and fasted, pleading to God to heal her. The woman was a devoted child of God, and everyone liked her. One day, at the hospital, members of her church surrounded her hospital bed, singing and praying for her. Suddenly, she passed away. When the people realized that she was no more, they began to cry uncontrollably, but a few minutes later, she woke up and began smiling at them. Everyone was astonished and happy to see that she had come back to life. Then, she waved goodbye to them, smiled again

Nothing Left Undone

and was gone for good. The church members, instead of crying this time, began to praise God for taking their sister to heaven. What an extraordinary way to return to God!

This event reminds me that death is, indeed, inevitable. I know some friends who once lived in the same community with me but who are now dead. My father, who took care of me years ago, is also dead. Death is real. Knowing that death is inevitable, the question we should ask ourselves is: "where do people go when they die?"

We know from the Word of God that life does not end here on earth, and heaven and hell are real. As children of God die, they will go to heaven while sinners will go to hell when they die. When God created us, He gave us freedom, and that freedom extended to the choices we make on earth. In Deuteronomy 30:15–20, we read that there is life, and there is death. There are descriptions of what we can do to inherit life or death. By the nature of God, He cannot force us to make our decision, but He continues to encourage us to choose life instead of death.

In the world today, however, there is a strong temptation for us to indulge in worldly pleasures. At some point in our lives, we need to have a serious discussion of how we intend to die, where we intend to go when we die, and how we intend to be remembered when we die. We should not allow death to meet us unprepared. To stand the chance of going to heaven, we need to evaluate our lives on earth and live a good life until the end, because what really matters is our state when we die.

Going to heaven can be likened to athletic events in the Olympic Games. During the Olympics Games, some athletes start the race strong, but somehow along the way, they fall off track, and those behind them finish the race. Some unbelievers, who later repent, may make it to heaven before some people who portray themselves as believers.

Since what matters is our state in the end, we must persevere until the end to obtain our glory in heaven. We should not allow earthly issues to distract us from finishing the race well. Our prayer should always be that we prepare for the hour of our death and return to our Creator in a state of grace— just as I believe my father did.

CHAPTER 11

Contentment Is Key to Harmony

I heard about a woman, whose trusted coworker had asked her to order a laptop worth one thousand dollars for him using her credit card. The coworker needed the computer urgently but could only find the brand he needed online. Since he did not have a credit card, he reached out to the woman to assist him to order the laptop, promising to pay her as soon as he received the computer. Due to the level of trust the woman had in her coworker, she never hesitated in ordering the laptop. In addition, she used her coworker's address for the delivery address of the laptop. Weeks later, she received an alert from the postal service, informing her that the computer had been delivered. A week later, her coworker had not told her he had received the computer.

The woman then contacted her coworker, and to her surprise, he had already connected the computer to the Internet and was using it. She then asked him about her money, but the coworker informed her that he did not have any money at the moment. He apologized for his behavior and promised to pay her the following month. Two months later, the coworker paid back only five hundred dollars, promising to pay the rest of the money the following month. Unfortunately, three months later, he had refused to pay the remaining balance, giving the woman one flimsy excuse or another.

The woman is certainly upset, as she had to pay interest to her credit card company on an item she never used. Today, the coworker is avoiding this woman, who is considering suing him to recover her money. Obviously, their relationship has been negatively affected. The coworker knew he didn't have one thousand dollars to purchase a laptop, but he went ahead and ordered it using someone else's money. He could have ordered a less expensive laptop, which he could afford, but he didn't. This did not have to happen had he simply cut his coat according to his size.

This incident reminds me of the contentment virtue my father instilled in me years ago. Mr. Nwosu lived a life of contentment. He was satisfied with the simple things of life and was always thankful. My father raised our family with what he had and never got carried away by material things. It is true that "the disease that kills a man begins with an appetite," as an African adage goes.

In the Bible, we are reminded of people whose lives were changed for worse due to their evil desires. Adam and Eve, for example, had a negative desire to be as wise as God. That craving led the serpent to tempt Eve and convince her to eat the fruit of the forbidden tree of the garden. She gave her husband, Adam, the fruit to eat, both of them, thus, disobeying God who loved them passionately. The

Nothing Left Undone

consequences of their disobedience were severe. In Genesis 3:16, we read that God said to Eve, "I will make your pains in childbearing very severe; with painful labor you will give birth to children. Your desire will be for your husband, and he will rule over you."

To Adam, God said, "Because you have listened to your wife and ate fruit from the tree about which I commanded you, 'You must not eat from it,' cursed is the ground because of you; through painful toil you will eat food from it all the days of your life. It will produce thorns and thistles for you, and you will eat the plants of the field. By the sweat of your brow, you will eat your food until you return to the ground, since from it you were taken; for dust you are and to dust you will return" (Genesis 3:17–19).

God also sent Adam and his wife away from the Garden of Eden, leaving them to provide for themselves.

To the serpent that deceived Eve into eating the forbidden fruit, God said, "Because you have done this, cursed are you above all livestock and all wild animals! You will crawl on your belly and you will eat dust all the days of your life. And I will put enmity between you and the woman, and between your offspring and hers; he will crush your head, and you will strike his heel" (Genesis 3:14–15).

Through the negative craving of Adam and Eve, they were destined to die. Their punishments extended to their generations in the world, but by the grace of God, we, as children of God, are saved.

Perpetua Anaele

A deadly desire also proved to be crippling for Samson in the book of Judges of the Holy Bible. Before Samson was born, God had already blessed and set him apart. In Judges 13:3–5, we read that the angel of the Lord appeared to his mother, who was barren, letting her know that she would bear a son and asking her to abstain from strong drink and wine. The angel also instructed her that her son would be a Nazarite unto God from the womb. Being a Nazarite meant that the child was to be set aside for God, and no razor should touch his head. As a Nazarite, besides growing his hair as a sign of his obedience to God, he was not to see a corpse or eat anything unclean (see Numbers 6:1–8). The child was to deliver Israel from its many years of captivity from the Philistines.

After his birth, Samson began to grow, and God blessed him and filled him with His Spirit (Judges 13:24–25). Later, in his life, Samson's supernatural strength from God enabled him to kill a lion with his bare hands (Judges 14:5–6). As an Israelite warrior, he became their judge for twenty years (Judges 16:31) and was very influential in fighting the Philistines who had held them captives for years.

As someone that powerful and special, one would think that Samson would be content enough to implement his Nazarite vows, but that was not the case; he had a negative appetite for beautiful women.

One day, he decided to choose a wife among the Philistines against his parents' wishes (Judges 14:1–3). He was disobedient to his parents given that as a Nazarite, he was

Nothing Left Undone

not supposed to marry from the Philistines, as they never served God and were enemies of the Israelites.

Later, up against the risk of being killed, he went to bed with a prostitute in Gaza (Judges 16:1-3). As if that was not enough, he was in love with Delilah, a Philistine woman. Before his relationship with Delilah, the Philistines had tried to kill him because of his constant attacks on them, but they were unsuccessful. Then, they learned of his relationship with Delilah and approached her, saying, "See if you can lure him into showing you the secret of his great strength and how we can overpower him so we may tie him up and subdue him. Each of us will give you eleven hundred shekels of silver" (Judges 16:5).

The eleven hundred shekels of silver were an offer Delila could not refuse, so, she decided to work for the Philistines to figure out where Samson's strength came from. On her first attempt to accomplish her mission, she was not successful: "Samson answered her, "If anyone ties me with seven fresh bowstrings that have not been dried, I'll become as weak as any other man" (Judges 16:7). She told the Philistines, and they brought her the bowstrings. She bound Samson with them while the Philistines waited in a room. After binding Samson, she alerted him of the presence of the Philistines. Samson broke the bowstrings as easily as possible, and Delilah accused him of mocking her for not telling her the truth of where his strength came from.

Delilah never gave up. She asked him again where his strength came from, and Samson lied to her for the second time: "If anyone ties me securely with new ropes that have

Perpetua Anaele

never been used, I'll become as weak as any other man" (Judges 16:11). She did the same thing. Yet, Samson was still strong.

The third time, Samson told her, "If you weave the seven braids of my head into the fabric on the loom and tighten it with the pin, I'll become as weak as any other man" (Judges 16:13). She did, but when she told Samson that the Philistines were upon him, he woke from his sleep and untied himself.

She then said to him, "How can you say, 'I love you,' when you won't confide in me? This is the third time you have made a fool of me and haven't told me the secret of your great strength" (Judges 16:15).

Being desperate, Delilah continued to pressure Samson to release the information to her. Finally, Samson said to her, "No razor has ever been used on my head because I have been a Nazarite dedicated to God from my mother's womb. If my head were shaved, my strength would leave me, and I would become as weak as any other man" (Judges 16:17).

When Delilah realized that Samson had told her the truth, she sent for the Philistines, informing them that he had told her all she needed to know. The Philistines brought the money they promised her. She then lulled Samson to sleep on her lap and called a man who came in and shaved off seven braids on Samson's hair. After that, she began afflicting Samson to test if he was still strong. Sure enough, he had lost his strength.

> "Then, she called, 'Samson, the Philistines are upon you!'
>
> He awoke from his sleep, and thought, 'I'll go out as before and shake myself free.'...
>
> Then the Philistines seized him, gouged out his eyes and took him down to Gaza. Binding him with bronze shackles, they set him to grinding grain in the prison" (Judges 16: 20-21).

The Philistines later humiliated him, offering great sacrifices to their god and rejoicing that their god had delivered Samson into their hand.

Later in the prison, Samson's hair began to grow. One day, as the Philistines were celebrating his defeat, they sent for him to entertain them. The Philistines then set him between two pillars, and he asked the servant holding his hand to ensure he could feel the pillars and could lean upon them.

The temple was full of men and women of the Philistines who watched while Samson entertained them. Samson then prayed to God, "Sovereign Lord, remember me. Please, God, strengthen me just once more, and let me with one blow get revenge on the Philistines for my two eyes" (Judges 16:28).

God granted his request by restoring his strength. Using his strength, Samson pushed the two pillars of the temple, collapsing the temple, killing the Philistines, and dying in the process (Judges 16:29–30).

Perpetua Anaele

This is a sad example of what a lack of contentment can do to people. Samson, despite his dedication to God, was brought down by a woman because of his destructive appetite. It is even more appalling given that Delilah had tested him three times and was unsuccessful. Without this negative desire, Samson would have left her after the first attempt. Samson had various opportunities to rid himself of his negative appetite, but he chose not to, and in the end, the talent God gave him was taken away from him, and he also died.

This is also true for our lives. God normally gives us many opportunities to get back on track from our sin. Even when we are in trouble, God, being ever forgiving, hears our prayers and helps us—the same way He heard Samson's prayer and restored his strength.

My father taught me to beware of having a negative appetite. This was why at about sixteen years old, when I drank alcohol, he was very furious with me.

In our world today, there are, unfortunately, instances of people dying due to one negative desire or another. I heard of someone who was so addicted to smoking cigarettes that she developed lung cancer. On several occasions, she would cough out blood and was rushed to the hospital. The doctors warned her to stay away from smoking; otherwise, her lung cancer would get worse. They prescribed her some medications, which she would adhere to for a week or two. After that, she would return to her normal smoking habit. This continued for years. During one of her hospitalizations, her doctors warned that if she tried smoking cigarettes again, she would die. She refused to listen. As she tried smoking one more time, unfortunately, she died.

Negative cravings also come in different ways. I have seen people who have a lot of material things, but they still complain that they do not have much. They end up doing unimaginable things just to acquire wealth, but in the end, they are never happy.

A lack of contentment leads to unhappiness. Years ago, I had a negative appetite for dresses. Every time I went to the store, I came back with a dress. For a week or two, after purchasing the dress, I would derive some joy, but weeks later, I would hate the dress and want another. This continued until I realized that I did not have enough space to store these clothes. I then decided to donate some to the thrift store to meet up with my poor behavior. Then, one New Year's Eve, I calculated how much I had spent all year purchasing clothes. The amount was so unbelievable that I needed to do something about it. In my New Year's resolution, I decided to stop the habit by buying only the dresses I needed—not the ones I wanted. Since then, I have been able to save some money.

My father taught me that contentment does not mean that people should not work hard. No, there is a need for people to work hard for a good cause. He advised that we work toward positive appetites, such as love, kindness, humility, patience, forgiveness, and other spiritual values. "If we have such values," he often advised, "we will most likely be content with what we have and be willing to share our resources with others."

The importance of contentment cannot be overemphasized. Solomon, in Proverbs 30:8, asked God to give him neither poverty nor riches, neither too much nor too little, but what was needful or necessary for him to survive. The trick is that as human beings, if we have more than we need, we become boastful of our accomplishment and may forget to recognize God who gives riches. Also, if we have too little, we may end up being upset and dishonor God. This is why Solomon asked God to give him the basics of life. That should be our prayer as well.

When I was growing up, my father preached that we-his children- share whatever we had with others. He said, "If you are eating, and your brother or sister has nothing to eat, share. Do not eat alone. If you have something, and your siblings do not have any, share."

My father was right. Think about it: we only need one pair of shoes at a time. What is the use of having closets full of shoes when our relatives and friends do not have any? We need to share. Some people have a yard full of different cars when they can only drive one car at a time. Wouldn't it be better if they were to share one of theirs with someone who had none? Some purchase all kinds of food and throw it away once it's expired. Wouldn't it be better if they donated some food to the homeless or to those who needed it?

From my life experience, we must give, or we lose. God has given us the world and expects us to give back in return. If we do not give back the right way by donating to charity or by helping a good cause, nature will, sadly, take it back from us in an awful way. This is the law of nature: we must give,

Nothing Left Undone

or we lose, and the more we give, the more we will receive. It is, therefore, in our best interest to give positively; otherwise, nature will take it from us negatively. I have heard stories of some people who refused to help those in need and later, they lost their money through unexpected income taxes, or other unforeseen circumstances.

I have also seen some people refusing to help their relatives to rise out of poverty. They forget that as long as there is poverty in this world, nobody is free. If we focus only on what we need, we could use the rest of our resources to help other people, and the world would be a better place for everyone. To those who render helping hands to those in need, please keep helping, as there is an enormous joy that comes with that.

It is true that we came into the world empty-handed, and as we die, we will return to our Maker empty-handed. It is only our souls that can last, and we should, therefore, invest in that which lives on. We can donate to our families and friends who are in the slums, and maybe with our help, they, too, can come out of the slums and start helping others. It is very important that we help others because the way we conduct our lives on earth will determine where we will end up when we die.

The Parable of the Rich Man and Lazarus in Luke 16:19–31 confirms how important it is for us to help those in need. In the parable, the rich man lived a flamboyant lifestyle. Lazarus, on the other hand, was a poor man who was laid at the rich man's gate every day. He was covered with sores, hoping to eat from what fell from the rich man's table. While he was there, dogs licked his sores.

Later, Lazarus died and was taken to Abraham's side, and the rich man also died and was buried. The dead rich man, while undergoing torments in hell, looked and saw Abraham with Lazarus at his side. Then, he said,

> "Father Abraham, have pity on me and send Lazarus to dip the tip of his finger in water and cool my tongue, because I am in agony in this fire."
>
> But Abraham replied, "Son, remember that in your lifetime you received your good things, while Lazarus received bad things, but now he is comforted here, and you are in agony. And besides all this, between us and you a great chasm has been set in place, so that those who want to go from here to you cannot, nor can anyone cross over from there to us."
>
> He answered, "Then I beg you, father, send Lazarus to my family, for I have five brothers. Let him warn them, so that they will not also come to this place of torment."
>
> Abraham replied, "They have Moses and the Prophets; let them listen to them."
>
> "No, father Abraham," he said, "but if someone from the dead goes to them, they will repent."

> Abraham said to him, "If they do not listen to Moses and the Prophets, they will not be convinced even if someone rises from the dead" (Luke 16:24–31).

This parable is in conformity with my father's teaching on sharing. One of the lessons for us is that we should learn to share with others and help those in need. If the rich man had taken good care of Lazarus, he would have probably ended up where Lazarus was.

The story also teaches us that God is not against rich people; rather, He cares about what the rich do with their wealth. The rich man did not go to hell because he was rich. He went to hell because he did not help someone in need. Think about it: Abraham was a very rich man; yet he was a friend of God.

My father always cautioned, "Given that the world is such that we cannot have everything we desire, there is a need for us to avoid bothering ourselves." Jesus in Matthew also teaches us to avoid worrying ourselves: "I tell you, do not worry about your life, what you will eat or drink; or about your body, what you will wear. Is not life more than food, and the body more than clothes? Look at the birds of the air; they do not sow or reap or store away in barns, and yet your heavenly Father feeds them. Are you not much more valuable than they?" (Matthew 6:25–26).

God loves us so much that He created us in His image. If He can take care of the birds of the air, He will definitely take better care of us. Why then should we worry over what we do not have?

Being content is one of the characteristics of a child of God. In his letter to the Philippians, Paul says, "I know what it is to be in need, and I know what it is to have plenty. I have learned the secret of being content in any and every situation, whether well fed or hungry, whether living in plenty or in want. I can do all this through Him who gives me strength" (Philippians 4:12–13).

Paul also reminds us in Hebrews 13:5 of the promises of God to those who are in need, "Keep your lives free from the love of money and be content with what you have, because God has said 'Never will I leave you; never will I forsake you.'"

In our human tendency, however, we often complain and blame God for not blessing us the way He has blessed our friends or neighbors. For example, we, at times, complain that we do not have jobs. Once we find one, we complain that it is tedious and pays little. We refuse to appreciate what we have, forgetting that nobody has it all. Instead of complaining about what we do not have, we should reflect on the things we have and thank God. When we do so, we will realize that we have enough—even if it is a word of advice—to help others, just as my father always did.

CHAPTER 12

BUILD A SOLID FOUNDATION

Therefore everyone who hears these words of mine and puts them into practice is like a wise man who built his house on the rock. The rain came down, the streams rose, and the winds blew and beat against that house; yet it did not fall, because it had its foundation on the rock. But everyone who hears these words of mine and does not put them into practice is like a foolish man who built his house on sand. The rain came down, the streams rose, and the winds blew and beat against that house, and it fell with a great crash.

—Matthew 7:24–27

A pastor in one of the churches I attended said he came across an interesting article about a man who had a big crack in the wall of his mansion. The man, being well-to-do, was planning a wedding for his daughter and had decided to host the event at his house to showcase his beautiful mansion.

Unfortunately, a month before the wedding, a big crack appeared in the wall in front of the house. He quickly sought the services of a builder. After receiving a huge sum of money from the rich man and repairing the broken wall, the builder informed him that the house was in good shape, and that he did not have any reason to worry.

Two weeks before the wedding, however, the crack appeared again, this time a lot more serious. The rich man was furious, and he quickly sent for the man to redo the work. When the man arrived, the rich man accused him of doing a lousy job for an exorbitant cost. He threatened to arrest the man if he did not fix the problem right away. The builder apologized, promising the rich man he would fix the problem. He did and nicely repainted the wall to the rich man's satisfaction.

Sadly, a week before the wedding, a still bigger crack appeared on the same spot. The rich man, out of anger, decided to seek the services of another builder. He informed the builder about the urgency of the issue, promising to pay him whatever amount he needed to resolve the issue before his daughter's wedding. The builder then began to do his job. He inspected the house thoroughly, and after about an hour of inspection, he told the rich man that the issue was not the crack but the foundation of the house. Adding that the foundation was poorly laid, he informed the rich man that no matter how many times he fixed the problem, there would always be a crack in the wall. He suggested that the rich man host the event in a different location and take his time to fix the foundation of the house.

The builder was correct. If the foundation of a house is poorly laid, the house cannot withstand any storm. Confirming the importance of a solid foundation in withstanding turbulence is a house known as the Sand Palace in Mexico

Beach, Florida. This house, in 2018, withstood Hurricane Michael—a hurricane that severely damaged most buildings in that town. The house, belonging to Dr. Lackey and his uncle, Mr. King, was constructed to withstand natural disasters, and when the storm came, it was the only surviving house in the town. Since the owners of the house laid a proper foundation by fortifying their house, it survived the storm while others collapsed.

Mr. Lawrence Nwalozie Nwosu laid a solid foundation of his life. Taking to heart Jesus' teaching in Matthew 7:24–27 referenced above, my father focused on what was important in this world—life with God—and lived a fulfilled and successful life. He understood Solomon's wise saying in Ecclesiastes 1: 2-4 (Revised Standard Version) that life without God is vanity: "Vanity of vanities, says the Preacher, vanity of vanities! All is vanity. What does man gain by all the toil at which he toils under the sun? A generation goes, and a generation comes, but the earth remains forever."

My father built his house on a solid rock, Jesus Christ. With Jesus on his side, every action he took, he invited Him to it, and He never failed him.

My father once told me that we, as human beings, are subject to death; it does not matter if we are rich or poor, educated or uneducated, young or old, influential or insignificant, we will die. For children of God, our souls will live forever with God when we die. For sinners, their souls will also live forever but in torment.

Perpetua Anaele

Having the mindset of all things being vanity, my father concentrated on his relationship with God. He modeled his character, uniting and reconciling people in the Lord. "Why fight over a piece of land, which you will not take with you when you die? Remember, nobody is buried on a football field. If you can afford a piece of land, great, but if you cannot, do not kill yourself over what you cannot afford," he often cautioned.

I bore witness to his humility, nobility, and selflessness. He recognized that it really does not cost a lot to pull someone out of misery, so he did what he could to ensure that he left the world better than it was when he was born.

Being a Catholic, he gave much of his time to serving God as an altar boy and later in his life, as a missionary interpreter. He was trained by Catholic priests, and he worked to mold characters in Nigeria, touring different communities and teaching.

My father encouraged us—his children— to take care of ourselves health-wise. He understood that health is an asset for success. This was why whenever we became ill, he took it seriously. He would rush us to the hospital and make sure we received the best treatment ever. He knew that if we were ill, we would not invest in ourselves, and the result would be a lack of success. He must have come to that realization when his six-year-old son mysteriously died in 1970.

My father had good friends in Nigeria, who were like-minded. He knew that good friendship is worthwhile and critical to a healthy lifestyle. He encouraged us to network with people who could help us grow positively as individuals.

I learned from my father that every human being is a builder. We do not necessarily have to construct houses, but as individuals, we each build our lives, such as our families, our careers, our relationships, and other things of life. In so doing, we need to realize that at some point in our lives, challenges or storms will test what we have constructed. It is not a matter of whether the challenges will occur. Experience shows that challenges are part of our lives; they will always come and go. This is why we need to prepare for them. It is very important, therefore, that as we construct our lives, we consider potential challenges or turbulences to ensure our lives will withstand the test of time."

Over the years, I have heard and seen people talking about how they could achieve healthy life habits. Some talked about getting enough sleep and not watching television before going to bed; others recommended combining exercise with healthy diets, such as reducing fat, salt and sugar intake. Still, others recommended activities, such as yoga, and other meditation techniques, to achieve inner peace and joy. While those activities and others have been documented as contributing to a healthy lifestyle, they are not long-lasting. I have seen people who gained weight after stopping their diets and exercise activities.

Such an experience has taught me that we need to embark on an action that can last forever. Given that everything in this world except God is vanity, there is a need for us to invest in the Word of God. With God as our solid rock, there is an assurance that we can survive whatever turbulence that comes our way. Being a child of God also disciplines us, enabling us to comply with activities that can bring us lasting peace and joy.

Through my father, I have come to realize that the only solid rock upon which we can build our houses on is Jesus Christ. My father encouraged his children and others to listen to the Word of God and put it into action. By so doing, we can achieve the legacies my father left us and even more.

On the other hand, if we build our houses on ground apart from Jesus, these houses will sink, disappointing us. It was my father's dream that we would excel more than he, and that we would live a peaceful life. He always wanted us to trust in God. I believe that only when we recognize the importance of living a simple and God-fearing life can we be likened to the wise man who built his house on a solid rock.

While my father is no longer with me, he inspires me every day to be a better person. He taught me to speak up when things are not right. He encouraged me to bring hope to the hopeless and to choose love instead of hate. My father taught me to forgive those who have wronged me and to discover my purpose in life.

As a decent man guided by faith, my father taught me to be closer to God, my Creator. He made me to understand that my actions will be my legacies. I saw in him the humanity in others, and the need to treat people as I would like to be treated.

Nothing Left Undone

Having been given so much, I am also giving back as I received. As a parent, I am setting for my children the same level of expectation that my parents had for me. With my husband's support, I am encouraging them to be brave, forgiving, hardworking, humble, kind, and responsible. They know the importance of family, and the need for family members to support one another and to share.

I am also teaching them that challenges are a part of our lives, and that they should embrace them without complaining. My children are aware of the importance of devoting time to serve God and man. They have participated in community service projects through their schools and on their own. I have taught them the importance of giving back to the society that has given them so much and to be thankful for whatever they have. It is, therefore, my wish that they will continue to carry on these important legacies and more to future generations.

When I was growing up, my father loved Psalm 128, which states,

"Blessed are all who fear the Lord,
who walk in obedience to him.
You will eat the fruit of your labor;
blessings and prosperity will be yours.
Your wife will be like a fruitful vine
within your house;
Your children will be like olive shoots
around your table.
Yes, this will be the blessing
for the man who fears the Lord.

Perpetua Anaele

May the Lord bless you from Zion;
May you see the prosperity of Jerusalem
all the days of your life.
May you live to see your children's children. Peace be upon Israel."

In those days, everyone in our family recited this psalm from time to time. As a child, I never paid much attention to it but as an adult, I strongly believe that my father achieved everything Psalm 128 promises those who serve God.

Although my father is absent in the body, he is present in the Lord, and like the Lion King, "he lives in me; he watches over everything [I] see, in the water, into the truth, in [my] reflection; he lives in [me]."

My father accomplished the goals Saint Paul wrote in his second letter to Timothy:

> "I have fought the good fight, I have finished the race; I have kept the faith. Now there is in store for me the crown of righteousness, which the Lord, the righteous judge, will award to me on the day— and not only to me, but also to all who have longed for his appearing" (2 Timothy 4-7-8).

The image in this book cover clearly depicts my father's outstanding persistence and endurance in the midst of hardship. During his ninety-eight years race in this world, he faced various obstacles, which intended to derail him.

Nothing Left Undone

When he encountered these bumps on the road, however, he activated his wealth of wisdom, trusted God, stood firm, followed the rules of the race, and persevered. In the end, he flew over every hurdle he met along the way, and crossed the finish line victoriously without any regrets. Therefore, I have no doubt that today, he is resting peacefully in the bosom of the Lord, receiving his crown of righteousness, and appreciating the fact that nothing he intended to do in this world was left undone.

ABOUT NOTHING LEFT UNDONE

We all face the challenges of life at some point in our lives. It could be in the form of a loss of a family member, job, relationship, or another life issue. These trials are a part of our lives and can happen without any warning. The coronavirus (COVID-19) pandemic is a typical example of what an unforeseen circumstance can cause.

At the time of publication of this book, almost every country has reported cases of the virus. Across the world, including the United States, life is not the same again. In an effort to reduce the spread of the virus, people are urged to exercise social distancing, avoid domestic and international travel, use personal protective equipment, maintain proper hygiene, get tested, and assist in contact tracing of possibly affected individuals. Despite these measures, millions of people globally have contracted the virus, and thousands have lost their lives. However, experts are predicting that this, too, will be over, and that we will be stronger than before.

Recognizing that positive things can come from even the worst situation, Perpetua reflects on the life and legacies of her father, who passed away in 2017. Despite her father's childhood adversity, he overcame various struggles and lived a fulfilled life. Therefore, regardless of the circumstances in which you find yourself, let her father's lessons on education, hard work, and resilience, among others, provide you insight on how to overcome such struggles and live a fulfilled life.

ABOUT THE AUTHOR

Perpetua Anaele is a talented author of an interesting educational, and inspirational memoir, Nothing Left Undone. Born into a loving nuclear and working-class family in Nigeria, Perpetua is the sixth of ten children. Following her marriage to an American Peace Corps Volunteer, Perpetua immigrated to the United States in 1994. With her spouse, later an American diplomat, Perpetua served at various United States embassies, including those in Bangladesh, Ghana, Mozambique, Rwanda, and Senegal. Perpetua and her family live in Maryland, United States of America, and she works in Washington, D.C.

Made in the USA
Middletown, DE
15 April 2021